Dissent and Empowerment

Dissent and Empowerment

Essays in Honor of Gayraud Wilmore

Edited by Dr. Eugene G. Turner

Witherspoon Press
Louisville, Kentucky

© 1999 Dr. Eugene G. Turner

Unless otherwise noted, Scripture quotations are from the New Revised Standard Version of the Bible, copyright © 1989 by the Division of Christian Education of the National Council of the Churches of Christ in the U.S.A. Used by permission.

The editor and publisher have made every effort to trace the sources of all quoted and cited materials included in this book. However, because of a variety of factors, that has not always been possible. If any copyrighted material has been included without permission and due acknowledgment, proper credit will be inserted in future printings after notice has been received.

Edited by: Dr. Eugene G. Turner
Project Director: David M. Dobson
Book interior by: J. Jarrett Engineering, Inc.
Cover design by: Peg Coots Alexander

First edition

Published by Witherspoon Press, a Ministry of the General Assembly Council, Congregational Ministries Division, Presbyterian Church (U.S.A.), Louisville, Kentucky.

Web site address: http://www.pcusa.org/pcusa/witherspoon

PRINTED IN THE UNITED STATES OF AMERICA

99 00 01 02 03 04 05 06 07 08 — 10 9 8 7 6 5 4 3 2 1

Library of Congress Cataloging-in-Publication Data

Dissent and empowerment : essays in honor of Gayraud Wilmore /
   edited by Eugene G. Turner. — 1st ed.
       p.   cm.
   Includes bibliographical references.
   ISBN 1-57153-015-0
   1. Race relations—Religious aspects—Christianity.   2. United
States—Race relations.   I. Wilmore, Gayraud S.   II. Turner, Eugene G.
BT734.2.D56   1999
   261.8′ 348—dc21
                                                      99—17504

Contents

Foreword

As a former student of Gayraud S. Wilmore during the years he was assistant professor of social ethics at Pittsburgh Theological Seminary in the late 1950s, it is a distinct honor for me to serve as editor of this book. The essays it contains were written by men and women who also learned from him under other circumstances and have since become his academic colleagues and friends. The title of this book, *Dissent and Empowerment*, refers to the primary thrust of Gayraud Wilmore's teaching, writings, and ministry, for he continues to dissent from conventional religiosity in order to empower the poor and oppressed who in turn must find the strength to swim against the tide of an unjust world for survival and liberation. Nevertheless, the title of this book is an apt banner under which these authors are more than willing to march, for most of the chapters express an angle of vision or a form of Christian faith that empowers those who exist on the margins where the battles against social and religious callousness and irrelevancy are continuously fought.

The idea for this *festschrift* in honor of Gayraud Wilmore originated with the executive committee of the National Black Presbyterian Caucus (NBPC) and among some staff at the headquarters of the Presbyterian Church (U.S.A.) in Louisville, Kentucky. Gay, as he is known by his friends, retired from the Interdenominational Theological Center in 1990 as a full professor of church history. It was the decision of the NBPC to invite a group of scholars to present papers at their 1994 annual meeting in honor of his long and distinguished career as a theologian, social ethicist, historian, and church activist. That was the year Gay retired as editor of the *Journal of the Interdenominational Theological Center*. Most of these chapters came out of that meeting and were recommended and initially gathered for publication by the Rev. Dr. J. Oscar McCloud, who at that time was executive director of the Fund for Theological Education in New York. Late in 1996 I took over editorial supervision of the project and the result is what you hold in your hands today.

This is not just a book about a person who has contributed to the liberation of African American and oppressed peoples in the United States and other parts of the world. More than a tribute to one person, it records some critical events that transpired between the 1950s and the 1980s when the churches of the United States and the so-called Third World were deeply involved in struggle.

This book addresses the protracted struggle for survival and liberation and, in direct and indirect ways, weaves through the following pages the passionate story of the action of God in our emancipation from every kind of oppression. Each chapter offers a different view of the forceful presence of the Holy Spirit in the fight for social justice, freedom, human respect, dignity, and equality in the United States. One internationally renowned contributor takes us across the globe to see these forces at work in the Republic of South Africa. Amazingly, these authors complement each other in a way that can only be accomplished in the finest literary sense when someone whose life and work, like that of Gayraud S. Wilmore, provides the occasion and the inspiration.

Dissent and Empowerment is must reading for those who would like to be well informed about the era of Civil Rights and the theological renewal that accompanied it. It should become required reading by professors who would like their students to understand one of the most significant periods in the life of American churches. If one was born between 1930 and 1959, he or she will want to read this book to get a view of the engagement of the Christian churches in the movement led by Dr. Martin Luther King Jr. If one was born between 1960 and 1980, he or she will find in this book a glimpse of a critical new consciousness that shaped the life and thoughts of their parents. I will give this book to my children—Peter, Paul, and Lennie Elizabeth—for that very purpose. They, and all of their generation, need to know how the Civil Rights movement consumed us and why their mothers, fathers, grandmothers, and grandfathers felt summoned by God to spend their lives in that memorable struggle for life and liberty.

The first chapter in this book is by Bryant George, a seasoned strategist of the urban mission of churches, foundations, and the federal government, who, probably more than anyone else, was responsible for Gayraud Wilmore leaving the seminary classroom in Pittsburgh to lead the United Presbyterian Church into the Civil Rights movement. His chapter, "A Firebell in the Night," is like a play-by-play of a football game with Gay Wilmore performing as the quarterback. The dynamics of the movement pictured by George are intriguing and will tell the reader considerably more than what the public knows about ecclesiastical responses to the crisis of the 1960s.

T. Richard Snyder, a professor of social ethics at New York Theological Seminary, writes on "The Protestant Ethic and the Spirit of Punishment." He explores the theological trance that he believes is induced by the way crime and punishment is connected to capitalism and racism. Snyder relates what is wrong with our criminal justice system to ill-conceived perceptions of biblical texts that would seem to give divine sanction to the way our society treats criminals.

James H. Cone, widely acknowledged to be the leading interpreter of black theology in academia, describes "The Vocation of a Theologian." His chapter provides sharp insights into the theological concepts that emanated from black oppression in the United States and the bravery required by anyone who aspires to be a black theologian.

Delores Williams, Cone's colleague in systematic theology at Union Theological Seminary in New York, in "Re/Membering African American Peoplehood—Resisting Its Dis/Memberment" presents an argument for the significance and necessity of recalling and putting together again—re/membering—the experiences of African American people. She shows how slaves and their descendants, though disabled by the lack of formal education, used wit and wisdom to relate God and the Bible to their daily experiences.

Thomas Hoyt's "The Ecumenical Legacy of Gayraud Wilmore: A Tribute to a Mentor" focuses on the honoree. Hoyt shows Gay's influence on the National and World Council of Churches and reveals along the way some interesting sidelights on the inner workings of those mainstream ecumenical bodies. Hoyt is a former professor of the New Testament at Hartford Theological Seminary, a leading ecumenist, and now a bishop of the Christian Methodist Episcopal Church.

Paul Griffin's chapter, "Theological Ideas Gone Awry: The Shaping of American Racism," presents historical insights into how the Christian religion in America doctrinally formed the concept and practice of racism that is a current scourge on the American society. A scholar in the history of religion, Griffin documents how eighteenth-century American Christianity intentionally created for whites a sense of superiority over blacks. The past and present roots and practice of racism are merged in this chapter. No religion escapes his penetrating scrutiny. Whether Christian, religious, or nonreligious, these chapters reward the reader with knowledge of roles religion plays in sustaining racism in American society.

Bishop Desmond M. Tutu, the retired archbishop of Cape Town, the Republic of South Africa, and chairman of the Truth and Reconciliation Commission for that country, speaks of the significance of the Bible and Christianity as a tool to subvert oppression in his chapter, "Why Apartheid Was Evil and Unbiblical." He states that, contrary to the view of the apartheid defenders, the Bible gave energy, power, and courage to the oppressed people in South Africa as it does for oppressed people everywhere. His chapter is sermonic and factual. It connects American racism with the racism of apartheid.

Catherine González, now a New Testament professor at Columbia Theological Seminary in Decatur, Georgia, was a Wilson College student who served under Gay's leadership when he was on the staff of the Student Christian Movement in the Middle Atlantic Region. In "The Quest for Holiness," she demonstrates how holiness was connected to a relationship with the neighbor as taught by the Benedictine order. She explores holiness as a community effort through which one only knows oneself as a sister/brother who belongs to the holy community.

The final chapter in this book was written by Gayraud Wilmore himself and is titled "Realism and Hope in American Religion and Race Relations." Here Gay gives us an introspective view of the major motif of his ministry—the encounter with racism from early boyhood through almost fifty years of leadership in the church and the ecumenical movement. This chapter depicts complex personal and group experiences that are a characteristic mark of his mind and writings over the years.

A brief biographical sketch on each of the contributors is found at the end of this book, including a somewhat more extensive biography of Gayraud S. Wilmore. The book also contains a bibliography of Gay's work, prepared by Dr. Joseph Troutman, librarian of the Interdenominational Theological Center, and study questions for each chapter developed and written by Arlene Gordon, Associate for Resource Center Development and Educational Ministry Advocates Support for the Presbyterian Church (U.S.A.).

It has been a great joy for me to join these distinguished scholars and church leaders in preparing this volume in honor of what the old-fashioned Presbyterians used to call "a Father and Brother" in the life and ministry of the Church of Jesus Christ. I know Gay well enough to know that he would not want me to make any more fuss than I have already made about his contributions to what African Americans and others have achieved in terms of justice-producing discipleship during the years of his influential ministry in the church and the academy. Moreover, these chapters by men and women whose lives he touched speak eloquently for themselves, and I humbly present them to the wide readership they most assuredly deserve.

Dr. Eugene G. Turner

1 | A Firebell in the Night

Bryant George

During the 1960s I worked as an urban strategist and policy maker for the Presbyterian Board of National Missions of the United Presbyterian Church (U.S.A.). I, along with several others in our church who were engaged in social ministry across the country, was a member of a loosely organized adjunct staff for the Presbyterian Commission on Religion and Race (CORAR), which Gayraud Wilmore headed. We all labored, under the aegis of CORAR, as a national network of both salaried staff and unpaid volunteers who, in one way or another, were trying to bring our predominantly white, middle-class church into the whirling vortex of the movement for racial justice.

Throughout those years, and particularly after the Commission on Religion and Race had its name changed to the Council on Church and Race as a result of a 1967 mandate from the church, I was probably in as good a position as anyone to observe Wilmore's prophetic leadership. Our offices in the Interchurch Center in New York City were only a few feet from each other, and we conferred and collaborated on almost every aspect of the work of the Commission from 1963 to 1972. Thus I wish to begin with a brief historical survey of the work of the Presbyterian Church in the Civil Rights movement under Gayraud Wilmore's leadership.

When he came to New York in 1963 to serve as the first executive director of the new commission—established that May by the 179th General Assembly in Des Moines—Wilmore was an assistant professor of social ethics at Pittsburgh Theological Seminary, ready to write his dissertation for a Ph.D. at Temple University. He had been a pastor, a member of the staff of the Student Christian Movement, and had served for five years on the staff of the Department of Social Education and Action of the Presbyterian Board of Christian Education in Philadelphia. He brought to his new position in New York a wealth of academic, administrative, and programmatic experience that qualified him to take the helm of the church in the area of race relations. In response to a broad consensus among the Negro (since the period being discussed used that term, I will use it here) leaders of the church, Dr. Edler G. Hawkins and I journeyed to Pittsburgh in the early summer of 1963 and talked Gay into leaving the classroom to help our church catch up with Dr. Martin Luther King Jr. Today, more than three decades later, I can look back on that one-day recruitment trip with some personal satisfaction.

2 | *Bryant George*

A Firebell in the Night

A firebell sounding in the dark of night is something one never forgets. Whatever else it may do, it breaks into your sleep, rudely jolts you into a nervous wakefulness, and immediately puts you on your feet. Gay Wilmore did something like that for the Presbyterian Church during the 1960s. He came on the scene when that particular denomination, not to mention most of mainstream Protestantism, was drifting from side to side on the bumpy road to racial justice. The church knew that something had to change, but had not yet mustered the courage and foresight of leadership to make the necessary changes that would throw its considerable resources into the fray that was, by 1963, raging in the South. The Presbyterian Church was waiting for leadership—in the Old Testament sense of the word, a prophet/judge—and Gay Wilmore rapidly assumed that role at the national level. As executive director of the Commission on Religion and Race he acquitted himself with the integrity, genius, and effectiveness that was called for if this new social action unit was to move the church from its half-somnolent condition on the fringes of the movement to full wakefulness at its center, where the action was. His actions left a permanent mark on the denomination.

The Battlefield of the 1960s

The Civil Rights struggle of the 1960s was caught up in the Cold War thinking of America. Anyone who sought radical change was considered a Communist. Real leadership in Civil Rights resulted in telephone tapping, secret mail openings, blackmail, or in the cases of Medgar Evers, Malcolm X, Martin Luther King Jr., and Bob Spike, a good deal more.[1] Negroes continued to do America's heavy lifting and continued to be marginalized. Negroes/Blacks/Afro-Americans sought change: an acknowledgment of the rightness of their cause, the justification of their complaints, public visibility, and the rights of first-class citizenship for themselves and those who would follow them.

Negroes and their few allies sought *radical* change. In the early 1960s, however, America had a right-wing president, John F. Kennedy, who believed with all his heart that Negroes should go slow—allow *"the thing"* to work itself out. The same could be said about his brother, Robert, the attorney general. (Robert's attitude changed after his brother's death, however.)

President Kennedy gave us no help at the beginning of the period, when attack dogs were unleashed on peaceful demonstrators; when county sheriffs

---

1. Evers was the assassinated leader of the NAACP in Mississippi. Robert Spike was the executive director of the Commission on Religion and Race in the National Council of Churches, which was created the same year as COCAR. He was mysteriously murdered in Columbus, Ohio, on October 17, 1966.

mercilessly beat demonstrators down to the ground and continued to beat them while they lay there; when buses carrying freedom riders to the South were burned or bombed. All the while, the White House stood silent. If any words were heard from that direction they were, "Go slow."

In the rural areas of the former Confederate States of America, the person to be dealt with at the county level was the sheriff. Sheriffs were not independent actors. They did the dirty work of the cadre of white leaders who hid out in their private clubs, segregated schools, churches, and homes in the Southern cities and hoped that their hired guns would be able to fight off these outside agitators, or Commies, or both, who they believed came to "upset our Negroes." These leading white people had at least one colored mammy (or her equivalent) who assured them that their Negroes were happy. Most of these mammys, of course, were balancing the need to survive with the need for change, and were playing on both sides of the fence. I take my hat off to them.

Discrimination: Segregation's Vital Lie

The "vital lie" that America believed during this period was that Negroes were happy with their lot. That is to say, the shared lie was that Negroes had no serious objections to being third-class citizens, having no vote in many places, segregated in almost everything everywhere, and generally understood to be morally and intellectually inferior to whites. They were, after all, children to be taken care of. "Gee, whenever I see them they are always singing and dancing, and most of all, grinning."

If Negroes looked to congress for help, they did not find the conservative Republicans who are in charge today, threatening to undo our civil and human rights and put our children in orphanages. In the early 1960s, the nabobs were not Republicans but Southern Democrats who dominated congress, opposed racial desegregation, rights for women, indeed, rights for anyone other than themselves. And such Democrats would filibuster at the drop of a sit-in. One Southern senator once read an entire book into the *Congressional Record* as a part of a filibuster to stall pending Civil Rights legislation. Here reigned those who were as determined as former Alabama Governor George Wallace that there would be "segregation today, segregation tomorrow, and segregation forever."

President Kennedy and his Department of Justice were indifferent. The Congress was hostile. The mass of white people, confused. The federal courts at that time were our only friends in government and, compared with all the other courts in the nation, they were generally fair, but also slow.

The Mainstream Churches in 1963

Throughout 1962 and 1963, students first, then Negro churches, then a new crop of Civil Rights leaders, started a drumbeat of demonstrations throughout the South to signal that Negroes were not willing to allow the system of discrimination and forced segregation to continue any longer.

The mainstream denominations were reeling under the pressure of these events, which they neither attended nor understood. This was, in part, because the churches sought peace and tranquility more than they sought justice. In fact, many church leaders stated that they believed the Negro had been "given enough" and should be satisfied. Meanwhile, a Negro could just as easily aspire to being governor of Mississippi as to be a synod executive in one of the nonsegregated synods of the Presbyterian Church. As a matter of fact, Negroes would become sheriffs, even mayors, in many small towns of the South before one would become an executive in a nonsegregated presbytery of our church.

Negro Presbyterians were showing up at Presbyterian churches in the South and were dragged away from the horns of the altar. Methodists, Baptists, and others were hauled off to jail exactly as though they had tried to desegregate the very own brothel of the chief of police. The Presbyterian Church (whether one speaks of the Northern or the Southern branch) was almost a totally segregated institution. Not only had a Negro synod or presbytery executive never been heard of, but rare was the Negro who served as a member on any board or agency of the church. At the local level, few Negroes were members of white Presbyterian congregations. There were, to be sure, segregated Negro judicatories in the South, and a segregated Negro "Council of the North and West" existed above the Mason-Dixon Line. But this Council, for all intents and purposes, was an entity of the Board of National Missions and was partly created in order for the board to incorporate its work with Northern Negro churches, even though those churches were technically members of white presbyteries.

Enter the Cubans

In the early part of the 1960s many Presbyterian church leaders would have rather passed large kidney stones than dealt with blacks' demands for Civil Rights. It was widely assumed that such demands disturbed "the peace and purity of the church." In this period, a large section of the white church in America—Roman Catholic and Protestant—was consumed by a Cold War fact: Thousands of white Cubans were fleeing their dictator in response to America's implicit invitation to come to the land of the free, get immediate citizenship status, good jobs, housing, and in many cases, adoption by the white congregation. The Presbyterian Church devoted a significant portion of the One Great Hour of Sharing offering to a resettlement fund for fleeing Cubans.

The church devised ways of getting around the United States government's embargo of funds going to Cuba and continued to fund work among the Presbyterian Cubans who remained on the island. The Board of National Missions opened a Special Office of Resettlement, and all aspects of resettlement were funded fulsomely. Few were the Presbyterian congregations that did not have at least one Cuban family as their ward, finding for them housing, clothing, schools, scholarship, and helping those who were professionals to leap the legal barriers that had been set up to keep professional workers from other countries from entering our markets and competing with Americans. The attitude of many in leadership, both in the church and the government, seemed to be "Cubans, yes; Blacks, no."

The United States government, of course, was behind this outpouring of Christian charity—cajoling, encouraging, smoothing the way for the churches to participate in the destabilization of Cuba. Millions of Presbyterian dollars and much effort was expended in this mission. Although their voices were scarcely heard, many blacks felt that these dollars were being subtracted from much-needed funds they might have been awarded for salvaging the witness of the Presbyterian Church in the inner cities while there was still time.

The Placebo Phenomenon

Plato said, "We can easily forgive a child who is afraid of the dark. The real tragedy of life is when men are afraid of the light." Beecher (1955) and White, Tursky, and Schwartz (1985) have shown in their studies that anywhere from one-third to two-thirds of all medical patients show marked physiological and emotional improvement simply by believing that they are being given effective medicine, even when that treatment is just a sugar pill or a ground boar's tusk. The Presbyterian Church spent untold thousands of dollars and untold hours of committee work "studying the race situation." They issued dozens of pronouncements on racial justice. By doing so, Presbyterians convinced themselves that they had solved the race problem. There was nothing left to do until it was time to issue the next placebo declaring that all was well with the soul of America. But placebos only work for a time. The hardest job that the Civil Rights movement had with the church was to convince Northern white Presbyterians that the Negro was indeed dissatisfied and that few, if any, of the demonstrations were the work of Communist outsiders.

Some Presbyterian leaders, when asked to desegregate all Presbyterian congregations, synods, presbyteries, colleges, camps, and conference grounds, all too frequently would say, "Most colored people want their own institutions, and in any case, we don't want to proselytize." The clear implication was, "If you don't like what we are, go somewhere else."

The Beginning of Change

The 175th General Assembly of the Presbyterian Church held its annual meeting in Des Moines, Iowa, on May 16, 1963. You almost have to be a

Presbyterian to understand how closely the voice of the Assembly comes to being the voice of God. At Des Moines it was composed of mostly white males, elected as commissioners from presbyteries, or regional groupings, from all over the nation. They represented the whole church in all deliberative, legislative, and judicial matters. In 1963, for the first time in the history of the church, a black person made a serious bid to be elected moderator (presiding officer) of the Assembly. He lost. I was the campaign manager for the candidate, the Rev. Dr. Edler G. Hawkins, and was told by white commissioners again and again, "The Church is not ready for a Negro moderator." Nevertheless, the pressure from outside the church and a great deal of insider politics made it possible to get the Assembly to invite Martin Luther King Jr. to speak at one of its plenary sessions. At the last minute, King was unable to attend because he was in the Birmingham city jail, from where he would write the now famous "Letter from the Birmingham Jail."

Edler Hawkins, pastor of the St. Augustine Presbyterian Church in the Bronx, was a giant in the denomination. The next year, 1964, he was elected the first Negro moderator of the church. At the 1963 Assembly in Des Moines, Edler Hawkins spoke in Dr. King's place. It was the right speech at the right time by the right man. Edler, on that occasion, accomplished more than Dr. King or any angel from heaven could have accomplished with the highest judicatory of the denomination. His speech was inspired by the Holy Spirit. Edler, a known quantity to the church, an insider who knew how to draw on the best talent in the denomination for help, electrified the Assembly. He called on the church not just to open its eyes to the realities of required change, but to open its purse to bring about that change—a change, a turnabout, from some of the iniquity of the past to an unprecedented decision to fund the radical changes that would be required in the future.

The Assembly responded. It authorized a national Commission on Religion and Race (CORAR) and put $500,000 aside for its initial budget. The Assembly gave CORAR authority to "immediately design a comprehensive strategy for the United Presbyterian Church's approach to race relations."

Enter Gayraud Wilmore

Obviously some of the changes that have taken place in the Presbyterian Church would have taken place without Wilmore, without CORAR, and probably with little leadership from the top. However, a great deal happened because of Wilmore's leadership through CORAR. He brought an enlightened vision of what the church could be if it were willing to concretize that vision. He brought a guiding image of a new future.

First, under Wilmore's leadership CORAR made the Presbyterian Church take seriously what was happening at that time in American society. It spoke from within the church to the church, about the sin of discrimination and racial separation. It issued clarion calls for change, and change was brought about in the body politic of the denomination.

Second, CORAR worked to put the Presbyterian Church in the forefront of the white mainline churches' leadership and involvement in the Civil Rights struggle.

Third, it awakened the church to the need for direct church involvement—the need for pastors and members of the church to join the sit-ins and demonstrations, and go to jail if need be, as part of their witness to the church's involvement in this fight for justice. Surprisingly, the church responded again, as it did in Des Moines, and hundreds of Presbyterian pastors and church members joined the demonstrations for justice and equality, albeit usually in towns other than their own. This was a mobilization of human resources from within our church that had never been seen before and hasn't been seen since. The Commission provided leadership and some funding, but the local churches and individuals followed its leadership by providing most of the money for their own travel to bear witness, go to jail, raise bail, and then return home to tell why they had to make this radical witness. This kind of direct action inflamed some members in the local congregations and presbyteries, but it converted others.

Wilmore and the Commission awakened the church to its sin of participation/profiting from segregation, changed the church's view of this kind of institutional racism, got the official publications of the denomination and its national leaders energized to espouse racial desegregation, mobilized individuals and congregations to join in the Civil Rights struggle, and changed churchwide funding patterns and hiring practices, an important structural readjustment in the institution itself.

Under Gayraud Wilmore's leadership the Commission channeled funds for racial justice initiatives and used them for fundamental changes in the church and society in general. Without leadership from the top, such changes would have taken decades to become reality. Changes at the top helped the lower judicatories of the church to attempt changes they had never had the will or courage to try before. The type of funding introduced by CORAR has helped to bring hundreds of black government officials into office today, compared to only a handful in 1963. With respect to the church itself, as a direct or indirect result of CORAR's activity, most Presbyterian retirement homes, and all the church's camps and conference grounds are now desegregated, and a number of blacks have served and continue to serve today as judicatory officials.

The Angela Davis Affair

CORAR, after its name was changed to the Council on Church and Race (COCAR), funded such courageous causes as the defense of Angela Davis, the black woman scholar who was an admitted Communist. Davis was on trial in California for murder. Members of St. Andrew Presbyterian Church in Marin County, California, felt that, based on what they had heard around town, Angela Davis would be railroaded and asked COCAR to help her get a fair trial. When COCAR made funds available, the white sector of the Presbyterian Church was enraged, believing that COCAR was trying to buy a Communist out of her guilt. As it turned out, thanks in some small part to the COCAR grant, Angela Davis received a fair trial and was later acquitted.

The rage of the conservative portion of the white Presbyterian Church was reflected in seven thousand written communications to the national church offices and to COCAR, objecting to the Davis grant. This material, consisting of six cubic feet of mostly bitter, some profane, all angry, objecting letters, overtures, and session actions, is available for students and scholars of the Civil Rights movement today at the Presbyterian Historical Society in Philadelphia, Pennsylvania.

The 1960s was a period of the breakdown of trust in government and in the faith black people had that white people would ever do the right thing by them in this country. The only black person who believes today that whites will invariably do right by blacks is Supreme Court Justice Clarence Thomas. (But that's another story.)

What we went through in the 1960s was a breakdown of the faith of many people in the American system. This logically brought about action by people with no faith in the system. The most visible of these people who lost faith were white peaceniks and black activists. But even very conservative blacks who had taught their children to obey the segregation laws and wait—"our time will come"—lost faith that the government of the United States would help that time to come. Many came to feel that they were ready for change even at the risk of jobs, income, reputation, or their very lives. In addition, because of the perennial violence visited on the black community by the white community, black people in the cities erupted in riots that were actually massive violent reactions to institutionalized violence. At one point, 125 American cities were under martial law. This simply meant that the local authorities could no longer control the violence that they had spawned.

COCAR was involved in trying to deal with both the short-term and the root causes and long-term consequences of violence in Watts, Newark, Detroit, Washington, D.C., New York City, and other major cities. Such involvement included sending its staff quickly to the scene to try to establish communication links between the rioters and the authorities to meet or at least discuss their demands. A lot of education took place in those riots, and the COCAR staff under Wilmore's direction was instrumental as a catalyst in the situation, meting out information and contacts that allowed this education to take place. No white/black forum had taken place in many of these communities, and from the point of view of the whites, there had been no need for interracial discussion about conditions in their communities before this time. Now all of a sudden it became imperative that communication take place. In these discussions, COCAR had the responsibility to relate to and have some influence on the Civil Rights groups, the most lively ones being in the South but the most volatile and dangerous being in the Northern cities. During this inflammatory period, Dr. King was not alone in his struggle to keep the movement nonviolent and focused on genuine, long-term goals for blacks and other minorities.

COCAR had to read the signs of the times and, like the story in the book of Daniel about the words written on Belshazzar's wall, interpret them to the church. The signs were there, but the recipients of the message understood them not. Wilmore and his people interpreted the signs of that day and spoke to the church about what needed to be done in the maelstrom in which it found itself.

Other Fellow Workers and Allies

Wilmore was joined in leadership in the church by a number of very important African American leaders in local congregations and judicatories who were working for change. There were far too many for me to name them all here, but I have to mention a few:

- G. Benjamin Brooks, a pastor in Tucson, Arizona
- James H. Costen, the present president of the Interdenominational Theological Center in Atlanta, Georgia
- Congresswoman Eva Clayton
- Cornelius Campbell
- H. Eugene Farlough, chaplain at the ITC
- Emily Gibbes, a retired Christian educator
- Walter Greene[2]
- Edler Hawkins
- Regional Hawkins, dentist and Presbyterian minister in Charlotte, North Carolina
- James Jones, synod executive
- J. Herbert Nelson I and Pickens Patterson—both pastors and Civil Rights activists in the South
- Mary Jane Patterson, head of the church's Washington office
- Bob Shirley, synod executive

———
2. Presbyterian elder Walter Greene deserves special mention. He was a layman of one of the Detroit churches who worked professionally in the field of equal employment opportunity. Green was authorized by COCAR to do a study of fair employment in the Presbyterian Church that led to important policy changes in church employment practices in the 1960s.

- Vera and Lee Swann, returned missionaries and Civil Rights activists
- Furman Templeton, former head of the Baltimore Urban League
- Hosea Williams, one of the top staff associates of Dr. King
- J. Metz Rollins, of the CORAR staff, now a pastor in the South Bronx
- Clarence Cave, formerly of the Board of Christian Education
- McKinley Washington
- Oscar McCloud, formerly of the COCAR staff, now associate minister of the Fifth Avenue Presbyterian Church in New York City

There are many others who in the interest of space must go unnamed. Of course, I must count myself in that special group that was close to COCAR and, like Aaron and Hur did for Moses during the battle with Amalek, held up the arms of its executive director in fair weather and foul.

One must mention also a very important group of white Presbyterian leaders, many of whom joined the battle at great cost to themselves. Whites at the national level who fought side by side with Wilmore and black leadership—as diligently, faithfully, and with as much to lose—include the following:

- Eugene Carson Blake, the Stated Clerk of the denomination
- Angie Gebhard, a lay leader
- Margaret Flory of the COEMAR staff
- Maggie Kuhn of the Board of Christian Education staff—later of Grey Panther fame
- Dean Lewis of *Church and Society*
- Dan Little, now acting president of McCormick Theological Seminary, Chicago, Illinois
- Stan Marsh III, a Texas banker
- Jack McClendon, a Washington, D.C., pastor
- Ken Neigh, at the time general secretary of the Board of National Missions
- John Coventry Smith, general secretary of COEMAR
- Don Smucker, who was sent to Mississippi to head Mary Holmes College and the Child Development Group of Mississippi (CDGM) when the Klan was killing people like him
- Bill Thompson, Stated Clerk of the General Assembly following Blake
- Philip Young, now a synod executive

Joining them were courageous pastors and laypersons in local congregations who were prepared to give their all. Some of these white Presbyterians gave up positions and alienated family and friends to make their witness for racial justice.

During this period there was also a growing group in the denomination made up of Hispanic, Native American, Chicano, Asian, and other racial-ethnic members of the Presbyterian Church who joined in the struggle begun by blacks. Together, in the 1960s, all these people brought about important changes in the way the Presbyterian Church understood itself; the way it framed its vision of the world and its mission in the world; and the way it used its physical facilities, hired its personnel, did its decision making, and spent its money.

The Church's Money

At the time of the 181st General Assembly (San Antonio, 1969), sit-ins in the offices of university presidents, corporate CEOs, government officials, and churches, had come into vogue. James Forman authored a document called "The Black Manifesto" that demanded massive reparations from the white churches and synagogues of America because they had profited indirectly from the uncompensated labor of enslaved Negroes. The Manifesto claimed that some five hundred million dollars was due from both the churches and society to repay Negroes for lost wages in the building of this nation for 246 years. In April 1969, James Forman's Black Manifesto was the most inflammatory document that had come before the powers that be since the days of the American Revolution, though, as a matter of fact, its actual dollar demands were modest.

During the San Antonio General Assembly, Forman sat in at the Interchurch Center on Riverside Drive in New York City, where the Presbyterian Church had its national headquarters. Forman occupied the office of General Secretary of the Presbyterian Board of National Missions, while another group of his followers sat in at Wilmore's office.

The San Antonio newspapers and many of the hometown papers of the Commissioners (delegates to the Assembly) were reporting these actions every day. Forman was on the telephone calling people on the floor of the Assembly from the General Secretary's office in New York City. The Assembly was up in arms. It was being picketed daily by right-wingers (renegade followers of the schismatic revivalist, Rev. Carl McIntyre) and was threatened with more sit-ins by left-wingers. People were asking each other, "What is this world coming to? What is this *church* coming to?" It was reported that some of the commissioners talked about buying baseball bats (commonly known as "toothpicks"), in case there was a sit-in at the General Assembly itself. Some were said to have asked for "toothpicks" so they could take care of the situation themselves.

The Presbyterian Church was literally about to tear itself apart. Some of the Commissioners probably thought and others said openly that "these niggers are attacking the most sacred of all our American icons: private property!" But

Wilmore and those working with him in San Antonio had the foresight and intelligence to use this rude intervention to get something done that was worthwhile. Forman was actually brought to the San Antonio Assembly. He talked about his "demands." Wilmore and others designed two responses for the Presbyterian Church that reflected pure genius. They prevailed on the Assembly and the boards of the church to set up two multiethnic, trans-boundary initiatives to help low-income, unfree, and minority peoples to help themselves. The first was the Presbyterian Economic Development Corporation (PEDCO); the second was the National Committee on the Self-Development of People (NCOSDOP). The latter was to be supported annually by a portion of the One Great Hour of Sharing offering (a once-a-year collection taken by almost all Presbyterian congregations).

The Presbyterian Economic Development Corporation

PEDCO was established immediately with a commitment of eight million dollars for capitalization. It never received another penny from the church. Actually, the money was never released to its board of directors. It stayed in the investment portfolio of the particular program board of the church that earned the money until the last minute, and then was released to the borrower on PEDCO's request. These funds came from the investment portfolios of the Board of National Missions, the Board of Christian Education, and the foreign mission board, then called the Commission on Ecumenical Mission and Relations. The fourth board of the denomination, namely Pensions, refused to cooperate.

PEDCO received the commitment of eight million dollars to invest in low-interest loans for minority enterprises. It was able to secure a once-in-a-lifetime find, a man named Milton Page, as chief executive officer. Page managed the operation from shortly after its inception at the 1969 General Assembly until shortly before its demise in 1988, after it had exhausted all its funds. When you make loans to very marginal groups, you ultimately lose all your capital. These groups by their very nature were high risk, and many could not pay the church back in whole or in part. PEDCO operated at a time when inflation rates hit 120 percent and interest rates were at 22 percent. Businesses such as minority-owned car-repair shops, beauty parlors, restaurants, meat-packing plants and shopping centers in the heart of the ghetto—rural and urban—would never have come into being without some kind of jump-start from some external source. For many, PEDCO was that source.

In addition to lending money to minority micro-businesses, it secured funding from the Ford Foundation, the Department of Transportation, and the Small Business Administration. The minutes of the 184th General Assembly in 1968 show that PEDCO leveraged approximately $120 million from other financial institutions for loans to minority businesses.

The loans went to a wide array of minority enterprises. PEDCO loans made possible the Harbison New Town Corporation in South Carolina; a Native American transportation company; Garland Foods, a black-owned food manufacturer in Texas; Martinez Aero Space Corporation in Louisiana; the Delta Wheel and Spoke Company in rural Mississippi (one of these limited-income owners is now a U.S. congressman). It financed hundreds of low-income housing units by putting up the pre-HUD costs of planning and specifications, legal accounting, and overhead expenses. Among the housing groups it assisted were the Southeast Alabama Self-Help Association (SEASHA), the Fort Green Housing Development in Brooklyn, New York, and N.O.A.H. in Cleveland, Ohio. It saved dozens of micro-enterprises from going bankrupt because they lacked adequate financial counseling. PEDCO's staff counseled with scores of companies that needed expert advice more than they needed cash. The staff contributed vital help to those companies in terms of preparing a financial plan, handling taxes, liabilities, marketing, and the other "how-to" concerns of micro-enterprises. PEDCO helped with cash-flow problems and both increased and protected the number of jobs that these minority companies made possible. When PEDCO was operative, it led in the field of minority enterprise financing. The Ford Foundation had a parallel program in its Program-Related Investment programs, and a few banks had minority windows. For the most part, however, the bank windows were shut tight in the early 1970s. Other church-lending programs for minorities were short-lived.

PEDCO was one of COCAR's greatest achievements, and it was under fire its entire life by right-wing Presbyterians and the publication *The Presbyterian Layman* because it was one of the Presbyterian Church's responses to Forman and the Black Manifesto, which they regarded as some kind of nihilistic attack against the property rights of Americans. Furthermore, editorials in *The Layman* objected strenuously to PEDCO using money from the investment portfolios of the boards, saying that that could not be done legally. But they were wrong. It was legal, and we did it with a clear conscience.

The National Committee on Self-Development of People

The NCOSDOP was another achievement of COCAR under Wilmore's administration. It was set up to give grants to self-help groups that were managed by low-income individuals. The committee makes funds available to self-help, people-oriented programs, in ghettos, low-income communities, *favellas*, native townships, and Native American reservations. It engages in direct funding to people who will help themselves, not to well-resourced groups that are going to help poor people, but to the poor and the powerless themselves. Since it was founded in 1970, it has made empowering grants of almost thirty million dollars—more than one million dollars a year. But it has leveraged many times that amount and has empowered literally scores of thousands of people and their civil sector organizations. NCOSDOP is alive today because it has had superior and consistent leadership and maintained meticulous bookkeeping. The Self-Development Committee has been blessed to have only two staff directors over this twenty-five year period. They were the best persons for the job—the Rev. St. Paul Epps and the Rev. Fred Walls. Walls, who continues to direct the program today, has assembled one of the most competent staffs in the church to run the program. It accounts to the General Assembly and to church members for every cent it receives and spends. It is an exemplar of openness and fiscal responsibility. And the One Great Hour offering allows it to be replenished every year. It has supported a broad array of American self-help groups and has even supported freedom movements in Southern Africa.

In 1971, shortly after its founding, there was a second big push for freedom in Africa, and the NCOSDOP either directly or through the World Council of Churches-supported organizations in the field, helped this freedom drive. This was at a time when South Africa, Angola, Mozambique, Namibia, and Zimbabwe were all fighting some of the worst colonialists/white racists on earth for their freedom. So NCOSDOP made grants (sometimes direct, sometimes through the World Council of Churches) for nonmilitary purposes—schools, hospitals, medicine, and the like—to the freedom fighters. Today the countries of Southern Africa and their people, now free, owe much to the Presbyterian Church and the insight and vision of its African American leadership.

Both PEDCO and NCOSDOP encouraged the development of counterpart presbytery and synod committees. NCOSDOP still has presbytery and synod level committees carrying on its work, which has magnified many fold and reaches down to the most needy communities of the United States and the Third World. These two agencies of the Presbyterian Church came out of the denomination's emphasis on religion and racial justice during the late 1960s. They will go down in church history as programs of a predominantly white and affluent church that, under the leadership of black men and women, leveraged millions of dollars for the empowerment of people of limited resources and minority communities at home and overseas—dollars the Presbyterian Church had not been giving before and, sad to say, may never give again.

Gayraud Wilmore, and those who worked closely with him, led a cadre of adjunct staff and a newly formed national commission made up of members elected at large from the church. He worked with these people, loved them, and educated them to the point that they moved with him, and together they successfully moved the Presbyterian Church. They brought about change within the denomination in its Christian education curricula, its mission programs, its hiring practices, its investment portfolios, and in many other areas. Wilmore and his staff helped to bring into existence the NCOSDOP, PEDCO, and a number of other initiatives, not as well known. The CORAR and COCAR worked in new ways to change how Presbyterians spent some of their money and how—after many years of charitable contributions to Negro education, Sunday school missions, and evangelism among minorities—they got into the business of grassroots empowerment. The NCOSDOP and PEDCO brought not just prayer and goodwill, but Presbyterian dollars, to help ensure power and liberation in low-income, minority, and freedom-seeking communities. These two organizations leveraged a multiple of millions of dollars worth of change and progress.

Gayraud Wilmore awakened the Presbyterian Church. With the help of those who supported and followed his leadership, he directed the church toward significant internal changes and taught it how to make a new, more enlightened witness in the fight for justice and self-development. When he retired from COCAR in 1972 to return to seminary teaching, the 188th General Assembly said of Wilmore: "He is one of our Lord's most faithful servants, a Christian prophet and social martyr." That may have been a little too thick a description of what Gay Wilmore did for the Presbyterian Church, but there it stands. I prefer to think of him as a firebell—a firebell in the night.

Questions for Thought and Discussion

1. Do you know persons who have left a permanent mark on the denomination as it relates to justice issues? What were these contributions?

2. Discuss the term "cadre of white leaders" and name people you consider who fit this description.

3. Discuss the term "playing both sides of the fence." Describe a situation that would be considered "playing both sides."

4. Discuss what it means to stall legislation. Identify instances within the Presbyterian Church that would fall into this category.

5. Discuss how African Americans and other racial-ethnic groups are or are not serving in leadership roles in presbytery and synod boards and agencies.

6. Discuss the statement "The Negro was dissatisfied." Is this still a reality or has the issue been resolved?

7. Discuss the statement "Most colored people want their own institutions." What are your feelings on this issue?

8. Do you feel that there is trust today between whites and racial-ethnic groups? Why or why not?

9. The statement was made that the Presbyterian Church was literally about to tear itself apart. Are these issues still around today?

2 | The Protestant Ethic and the Spirit of Punishment

T. Richard Snyder

OUR NATION IS experiencing an epidemic of punishment that is approaching genocidal proportions. A recent study conducted by the Sentencing Project in Washington, D.C., indicates that one out of every three black men between the ages of twenty and twenty-nine is either in jail, paroled, or on probation.[1]

During the thirty years that I have worked with Gayraud Wilmore in his varying capacities as a church executive, seminary dean, and activist–scholar of African American religion, he has had a compelling and consistent concern for the downtrodden, dispossessed, and discarded—particularly the disproportionate number of African Americans and other people of color who are trapped in the United States penal system.

I have come to share that concern. For twelve years now I have been teaching in the New York Theological Seminary's Master of Religious Studies degree program at Sing Sing prison, a pioneering intramural educational program designed for long-term prisoners brought together at Sing Sing from prisons throughout New York State. It has been for me a true love/hate experience. The classes have been exciting, challenging, deepening. The men's motivation and surprising brilliance often match and sometimes outstrip those of the best graduate students I have worked with at various seminaries and universities. Discussions are vigorous, contested, and of ultimate importance. I *love* going there.

But notwithstanding the richness of the experience, my chest tightens and I find myself depressed every time I enter those gates, go through that rigid security check, and, escorted by some tight-lipped guard, walk the half mile through drab, echoing halls. I peer out windows that reveal razor wire atop every wall. I stride stiffly through as many as eleven steel gates that slam shut behind me. Finally, I arrive in a basement room that doubles as a theological library and classroom into which fourteen or fifteen men and a visiting professor are crowded for a day of study and instruction. Repeating the same processes in reverse upon leaving the prison at the end of the day, I cannot wait to get out. I *hate* going there.

The men are numbers, not names. They are often unprotected from the bru-

---

1. *The New York Times*, Week in Review section, p. 2, Oct. 8, 1995.

tality meted out by guards and other prisoners. Rape and other forms of violence are everyday occurrences. Their surroundings are sterile. Some of the guards speak hatefully of the prisoners. "They're garbage!" "We should throw away the keys and leave these animals to rot!" Venom and vengeance fill the air.

This spirit of punishment is not confined to our prisons. It pervades the wider society. Motorists are shot on Texas highways for cutting in line or not driving fast enough. Media hate mongers call for tougher sentences for crime and are cheered by the masses. A babysitter throws an infant across the room for pulling her hair—the child dies. Former President Ronald Reagan plays the role of a schoolyard bully with his challenge "Make my day." We are a nation quick to punish those whom we judge to be offensive or bothersome.

Perhaps nowhere is the spirit of punishment more evident than in our response to crime. Walter Berns notes that after a period of decline, punishment is again on the rise. It is a trend that has been gaining momentum in recent years. The 1976 report of the Committee for the Study of Incarceration spoke of "a renewed interest in the old fashioned view (a view never abandoned by most citizens) that criminals deserve to be made to suffer in proportion to the suffering they have inflicted on others."[2]

The state of New York's mandatory sentencing for the possession of four ounces or more of a narcotic is part of the attempt to get tough on crime. For first-time offenders, it is fifteen years to life; repeat offenders, twenty-five years to life. There can be no mitigating circumstances. The result has been an explosion of prisoners and no abatement of drug use. Some innocent persons have been caught in the trap of this impliable law. In particular, many poor women from developing countries who have been forced or duped into becoming couriers of illegal drugs have been incarcerated. These so-called drug mules are often totally unaware that they are carrying drugs—but they are arrested and imprisoned nonetheless.

Throughout the nation, the number of people imprisoned has mushroomed. In California alone, the number of men and women in correctional facilities rose from 13,169 in 1952 to 97,309 in 1990, an increase of over 700 percent.[3] The number of prisons built has increased dramatically, despite the fact that one cell often costs in excess of $100,000. The Justice Departments' Bureau of Justice statistics reports that between June 1994 and June 1995 "the prison population rose by at least 10 percent in almost half the states . . . Texas had the biggest gain, at nearly 27 percent . . . "[4]

———
2. Walter Berns, "Retribution and Punishment," in *Issues of Criminal Justice*, edited by Fred E. Bawman and Kenneth Jensen (Charlottesville, VA: University of Virginia Press, 1989), p. 7.

3. Lawrence M. Friedman, *Crime and Punishment in American History* (New York: Basic Books, 1993), p. 461.

4. *The New York Times*, Oct. 4, 1995.

In 1976, the Supreme Court voted to reinstate capital punishment and as of this writing it is now on the books in thirty-eight states. During the last seventeen years, 202 persons have been executed. A few years back, when the state of Washington reinstated the death penalty, people gathered in the city of Walla Walla to celebrate the first hanging. They cheered and set off fireworks.

Unfortunately, this "toughening" seems not to have assuaged our national thirst for vengeance. It has only whetted our appetites for more. In the fall of 1993, the United States Senate passed an Omnibus Crime Bill that allocated billions of dollars for new prisons and 100,000 additional police officers. In a series of approved amendments to that bill, children could not be tried as adults for many federal crimes, membership in a street gang would become a federal offense, forty-seven crimes would be punishable by death, and " . . . anyone convicted of a third felony would automatically receive life in prison without parole, regardless of the offenses."[5] And so it goes.

Perhaps this litany is too familiar to all of us. But what lies behind it? Certainly there is no single cause, and any direct causal relationship is finally impossible to establish. Nonetheless, it is important to try to understand what drives our nation to increased vengeance on its citizens, wayward or innocent, as the case may be.

Several possible answers immediately came to mind. First, there is the sheer volume of crime, which has caused widespread fear and rage. In 1990, 2.3 million Americans were victims of violent crime, according to figures compiled by the Bureau of Justice Statistics. The total number of crimes, including thefts, was nearly 35 million.[6]

The small decline in the number of violent crimes in recent years may or may not constitute a trend. But even if there is a decline in numbers, an inescapable consideration is that the amount is still overwhelming. Second in importance is the increasingly random nature of much crime. Innocent victims on commuter trains, in restaurants, or just glancing out of their windows are targeted or caught in the crossfire. Such randomness significantly raises the level of apprehension for everyone and makes the measures we take to protect ourselves seem ineffective. The response to both of these factors has been a cry for punishment.

Then there is the media. How many times must we see the Indians portrayed as brutal savages so we can cheer with a good conscience for the cowboys? How many violent police stories must we watch before we find ourselves eerily exhilarated by the violence meted out to the "bad guys"? How many news stories of random, violent crimes can we take without becoming paranoid?

Underlying these and other reasons are the class and racial interests that

---

5. An editorial in *The Nation*, Dec. 6, 1993, p. 677.

6. Friedman, *Crime and Punishment in American History*, p. 451.

have turned prisons into the warehouses for the unwanted and increasingly un-needed underclass of our society. Not coincidentally, the majority of those imprisoned are people of color, predominantly African American and Latinos.[7] When we look at the percentage of white men to black men, the figures become even more stark. About 1 in every 15 black men is in prison or in jail, compared to only 1 in every 100 white men.[8] But it would be irrational to attribute the entire problem to some simplistic economic or racial determinism. There is a role that culture and ideas play in the shaping of social policy and it is usually much more complex and less direct or intentional than any simple determinism would allow. Or to put the matter another way, the racism and class divisions that characterize our society and that we see played out in our penal system are reinforced, encouraged, rationalized, and stimulated by ideas and cultural aspects that are often imperceptibly linked.

Despite the fact that our nation has been built on racism and continues to operate in both a covertly and overtly racist manner, such an allegation does not necessarily help us to understand either the complexities of this reality or the way out. In fact, some Euro-Americans with whom I speak do not think of themselves as racist and are unaware of how certain arrangements benefit them because of their race and at the same time oppress others because of their race.

Such a lack of awareness is, of course, no excuse. There can be no innocent ignorance any longer. But the fact that these whites are not innocent does not change the fact that they are often essentially unaware of how our society operates when it comes to racism. And this lack of awareness is as pronounced within our churches as it is in the larger society.

As a theologian and an ethicist, I have been interested in whether and how our theology may unwittingly play into the hands of racial, class, and other divisions. The spirit of punishment that permeates American society may offer some clues. It is my contention that this spirit of punishment, which so disproportionately falls on the poor and people of color, is a cultural dynamic at least reinforced by, and perhaps to some extent rooted in, common-sense Protestant theology.

Max Weber's study of the relationship between Protestantism and capitalism[9] provides an important clue for understanding the spirit of punishment today that I believe fits well with a class/race analysis. Weber's basic point—that Protestantism's notion of the call provided a rational justification for the making of profit and led to behaviors conducive to such an enterprise—offers a

---

7. For a full documentation of this thesis, see Jeffrey Reiman, *The Rich Get Richer and the Poor Get Prison*, 3rd ed. (New York: Macmillan, 1990).

8. *The New York Times*, Dec. 14, 1995.

9. Max Weber, *The Protestant Ethic and the Spirit of Capitalism*, translated by Talcott Parsons (New York: Charles Scribner's Sons, 1958).

fascinating glance into the interplay of religion and the economic arena. Despite criticisms of his method, his limited recognition of other factors also at play, and his selective use of the English Puritan form of Calvinism, Weber's thesis remains central to the debate. The most important element of this thesis, for our purposes, is the *unwitting* nature of religion's impact on the economic culture and spirit. Despite the consciously religious intentions of its doctrines, the consequences of Calvinism for the secular public arena were far-reaching.

It has always been that way. Religious ideas and practices frequently have indirect, subtle, and unintended impact on the broader culture. Darrell J. Fasching's study of the Holocaust shows that the foundation for the anti-Jewish spirit that swept Europe lay in the theological notion of supersession that, although never intended as a support for genocide, made genocide thinkable.

> Based on my myth of supersession, which has its roots in the New Testament literature, the Christian claim has been that Christ has brought a "new covenant" that replaces the old (e.g., Hebrews 8). Therefore the people of the Mosaic covenant have no right to exist as God's chosen people. By claiming that election was transferred from the people of Israel to the community of the new covenant, Christians have engaged in a process of spiritual genocide. . . . The step from such spiritual genocide to physical genocide—from "you have no right to exist as Jews" to "you have no right to exist" is a step prepared by Christian *religious* anti-Judaism and carried out under Nazi *secular* anti-Semitism.[10]

Walter Wink, in the first of his trilogy of the Principalities and Powers, has uncovered the ways in which the spirit of an age was part of the biblical understanding. Drawing on Michael Foucault's metaphor of "epistemological space specific to a particular period," Wink notes that "what we are dealing with here is . . . the unconscious presuppositions and worldview of an entire era."[11]

Cornel West has documented the often-unconscious process of hegemonic collusion in his study of the genealogy of modern racism. He traces the way in which the scientific stance of observation, coupled with the Greek notion of beauty, went hand in hand with a developing deprecation of blacks and the rise of the assumption of white supremacy. The important thing to note about this process is that " . . . the initial structure of modern discourse in the West 'secretes' the idea of white supremacy."[12] West's use of the word *secretes* is especially important. To *secrete* may mean either to conceal or to release, as in a poisonous gas. In the case of racism, both meanings are accurate. White ideology

---

10. Darrell J. Fasching, *Narrative Theology After Auschwitz: From Alienation to Ethics* (Minneapolis: Augsburg Fortress Press, 1992), p. 21.

11. Walter Wink, *Naming the Powers: The Language of Power in the New Testament* (Philadelphia: Fortress Press, 1984), p. 7.

12. Cornel West, *Prophecy Deliverance! An Afro-American Revolutionary Christianity* (Philadelphia: The Westminster Press, 1982), p. 48.

is usually overt and often so palpably obvious that it sometimes is labeled "propaganda." Cultural influences are often so subtle as to go unnoticed. They are often concealed, or at least taken for granted. Nonetheless, they deliver an impact—they release a spirit. Hegemony often involves indirect and often obtuse linkages rather than immediately evident correlations.

My thesis is that there is a subtle, unintentional correlation between the dominant Protestant understanding of grace and the spirit of punishment in our society, a spirit that furthers the demonic powers of racism.

When I speak of the Protestant understanding of grace it should not be presumed that I mean to limit those who operate by that theology only to Protestants. As the advertisement for Levy's Jewish Rye bread says, "You Don't Have To Be Jewish To Love Levy's." And you don't have to be a Protestant Christian to know the song "Amazing Grace," or to be infused with a Protestant notion of grace.

My wife Carole and I once spent Christmas Eve on a train traveling from New York to Florida. At midnight in the bar car, we were singing carols. Many of the passengers didn't know the words, but when we sang "Amazing Grace," almost everyone in the car—Christians, Jews, and non-religious—joined in. The lyrics as well as the music, despite their origin and formal theological intent, are part of our culture. I even heard it played between innings at a Philadelphia Phillies baseball game recently.

And herein lies an important truth. Much of Christian theology, particularly in its Protestant form, has become part of the air we breath in the culture of North America. In the case of the doctrine of grace, that may be very dangerous. The commonly accepted Protestant notion of grace suffers from two critical distortions, each of which is reinforced within the first stanza of the song "Amazing Grace."

Amazing Grace, how sweet the sound,
    that saved a wretch like me.
I once was lost, but now am found,
    was blind, but now I see.

Moreover, each of these distortions has contributed to the spirit of punishment.

The first distortion is an understanding of wretchedness whose corollary is an absence of creation grace. The second is an individualized and a-historical notion of redemptive grace. Because of Protestantism's high doctrine of sin ("a wretch like me," with its emphasis on the Fall and the concepts of original sin and total depravity), it is difficult to find within Protestantism an affirmation of the intrinsic beauty, goodness, and worth of all creation. Granted that John Newton, who penned the hymn, was a profligate and a slave trader. But was he nothing more than a wretch? Are we nothing more than wretches by (fallen) nature? So, within mainstream Protestantism, it would often seem. Whatever grace creation once possessed has been lost with the Fall. Only in redemption can grace be restored.

My daughter, who is not noted for the frequency of her church attendance, was unaware that she was paraphrasing Walter Rauschenbusch when she complained that the pastor of her in-law's church "feels he has to tell us every week what terrible sinners we are in order to make God look good."[13]

This refusal to see human goodness and capacity for truth within fallen humankind is endemic to much of Christianity, particularly Euro-American Protestantism. It finds its earliest champion in St. Augustine and is picked up with a vengeance by Calvin, Luther, and Barth.

I do not wish to fall into the error of which Matthew Fox has been accused by Rosemary Radford Reuther, namely the distortion of both those who fit his agenda and of the "bad guys" who espouse a fall/redemption spirituality.[14] Fox's contribution lies not in terms of what redemption requires (in that regard I consider him simplistic), but rather in what I consider his accurate recovery of a central tradition that critiques the dualism present within the dominant fall/redemption motif.

There is a counter tradition that Reuther, in the same article, acknowledges to be central in Christianity. One of the most thorough tracings of this tradition is James Carpenter's *Nature and Grace*. Juxtaposing Ireneaeus and the Eastern theologians with Augustine, Carpenter concludes that they taught that the image of God had not been lost.[15] In that same vein, over fifty years ago James Muilenberg's biblical study of the *imago dei* found that nowhere in Scripture do you find such a pessimistic interpretation of the Fall as that held by Luther and Barth.[16] Peter Paris has documented this same tradition within the black churches. Although slavery and racism forced black preachers and theologians to acknowledge the radical nature of sin, they were somehow able to keep sight of the fundamental presence of the *imago dei*. This recognition enabled them to affirm the kinship and equality of all people.[17]

This core tradition has been lost or distorted by much of Protestantism as we have succumbed to a view of wretchedness that eliminates the image of God, denying the beauty, truth, goodness, and worth present in all creation. And the consequences have been severe.

---

13. Walter Rauschenbusch, *A Theology for the Social Gospel* (Nashville: Abingdon Press, 1978), p. 39.

14. Rosemary Radford Reuther, "Has Matthew Fox Oversimplified Creation Spirituality?" *In the Catholic World,* July/Aug., 1990.

15. James A. Carpenter, *Nature and Grace: An Integral Perspective* (New York: Crossroad, 1988), chapter 2.

16. James Muilenberg, "Imago Dei," in *The Review of Religion*, May, 1942.

17. Peter J. Paris, *The Social Teaching of the Black Churches* (Philadelphia: Fortress Press, 1985), pp. 11 and 15.

The first consequence is one that we are becoming increasingly aware of, namely, the destruction of nature. James Nash points out the complicity of Christian theology in nature's demise through our treatment of nature as subsidiary to or merely as a function of human history. Summing up, he writes:

> For most theologians—Augustine to Luther, Aquinas to Barth, and the bulk of the others in between and before and after—the theological focus has been on sin and salvation, the fall and redemption, the divine-human relationship over against the biophysical world as a whole. The focus has been overwhelmingly on human history to the neglect of natural history. . . . and thereby gave tacit (rarely explicit) permission for environmental destruction to proceed as an ultimately and morally immaterial matter.[18]

Sallie McFague's critique of Christianity's failure to recognize the world as God's body because of its hierarchical and patriarchal orientation[19] and Thomas Berry's call for the recovery of the numinous state of matter,[20] each further substantiates the radical dualism of Protestantism's fall/redemption theology and its consequences for the environment. These devastating consequences to the environment are also carried into the arena of human interaction as we make the kind of distinction we do between "the fallen" and "the redeemed." A great gulf is fixed, as between Lazarus and the rich man in Jesus' parable (Luke 16). The difference between the fallen and the redeemed is literally as severe as that between life and death. Fall and redemption are classifications of two realities of different states of being.

Herein lies the problem. When we see the world as containing two realities of different states of being, it is an easy step to expand the classifications of two different beings in creation. Why not male and female, white and black, native and foreigner, straight and gay, criminal and upright citizen? I am not suggesting an historical sequence, but an oscillating movement, a mutual reinforcement among our classifications. People who see the world in terms of white superiority and black inferiority certainly are ready subjects for a dualistic theology of fall and redemption, or vice versa.

To classify persons is to treat them as objects. That is the lesson of the Gospel story of the man born blind in John 9. The disciples asked, "Rabbi, who sinned, this man or his parents, that he was born blind?" (John 9:2). The automatic assumption was that sickness was the result of sin. Instead of sorrow for his blindness, the disciples related to the blind man as an object whom they classified—a sinner. They talked *about* the man and pointed to him. In contrast,

---

18. James A. Nash, *Loving Nature: Ecological Integrity and Christian Responsibility* (Nashville: Abingdon Press, 1991), p. 72.

19. Sallie McFague, *Models of God: Theology for an Ecological Nuclear Age* (Philadelphia: Fortress Press, 1987).

20. Thomas Berry, *The Dream of the Earth* (San Francisco: Sierra Club Books, 1990).

Jesus talked *with* the man and touched him. The disciples did not deal with the blind man as a person. They dealt with him as a classification.

That is what we in the United States have done to persons who commit crimes. Or at least to certain persons who commit crimes, namely, people of color and those in the lowest ranks of our economic system. The *New York Times* business section carried a lead article in which the writer pointed out the widely varying assumptions people have about street criminals as compared with "suite" criminals. Concerning the latter (those who commit white-collar crimes) he tells us that many people believe that "such violators [white-collar criminals] are basically good people who stepped over the line but are not really criminals."[21]

The majority of prison inmates in the United States are people of color and/or people from lower socioeconomic classes. And for them, the treatment is largely one based on the classification of wretch, of non-person. Several examples will serve to make this point. The thirty-five-year-old Jamaican man who murdered six people and wounded seventeen on a Long Island commuter train was called an "animal" by a leading police official. Even given the legitimacy of the official's rage and the horror of the crime, the man is not an animal. He is God's child, our brother. He is pathologically sick and in need of help, perhaps in need of being locked up to protect others. But he is not an animal.

When, on one occasion, I tried to send flowers to a prisoner who had been hospitalized, an officer not only told me that the prisoner was not permitted to receive flowers, but that he wouldn't appreciate them anyway. I responded with incredulity, "But everyone likes flowers. He's a person, too." "No, he's *not*," was the officer's retort, "he's a criminal!"

The chilling introduction to *Life Sentences: Race and Survival Behind Bars* provides a sobering account of our potential inhumanity to criminals when we treat them as objects and not as persons. Sam (an alias), the Louisiana State executioner, has killed nineteen people in the electric chair, receiving four hundred dollars for each execution. Noting the impersonality and efficiency of the killings, the authors quote Sam as saying, "There's nothin' to it. It's no different to me executing somebody and goin' to the refrigerator and getting a beer out of it."[22]

Sam's matter-of-factness is different only in degree, but not in kind, from many people with whom I've come in contact. The truth is that for many in our society, prisoners are considered toxic waste: Whatever value they may have had in the past is now absent. They are fit for nothing. Even keeping them around

---

21. *The New York Times*, Oct. 3, 1993, section 3, p. 1.

22. Wilbert Rideau and Ron Wikberg, *Life Sentences: Race and Survival Behind Bars* (New York: Times Books, 1992), p. 5.

is increasingly problematic. If we could bury them and forget them, we would do so without remorse. It is an easy step to treat people as toxic waste when they are considered graceless wretches, devoid of any beauty, goodness, or worth. Our punitive response to crime is significantly reinforced by the loss of the sense of creation grace.

The second distortion of the mainstream Protestant theology of grace is that redemptive grace is understood almost exclusively in individualistic, internalized, nonhistorical terms.[23] Such an approach ignores the full complexity of grace that is needed for holistic redemption to occur. The consequences of this truncation are, first, that the larger circle of complicity is denied and the social ramifications of redemptive grace are lost; and second, that selected scapegoats are targeted for vengeance.

At this point it is important to recognize that prisons are largely not about redemption. They are, as I am insisting, about punishment. In a December 1993 interview, the attorney general of the state of California cited four purposes of prisons: retribution, punishment, incarceration, and deterrence.[24] Absent from his list was any mention of rehabilitation or redemption. In fact, the rehabilitative ideal has seldom been at the core of our penal system, despite such euphemistic nomenclature as "penitentiary" and "correctional facility," each of which implies the possibility of a fresh beginning, of starting all over again, of redemption. However, in those rare cases in which redemption is attempted, it is doomed to fail so long as it is taken for granted that redemption is an individual matter.

When the Bible speaks of the sins of the parents being visited to the third and fourth generation (Num. 14:18), it recognizes a truth that has been consistently ignored in the Western church and society. Sin is infectious and spreads like an epidemic. This, it seems to me, is a far more accurate understanding of the Fall and the radical nature of sin than the Augustinian/Reformed notion of original sin. Sin is radical and pervasive. Its roots are deep and its branches extensive.

It is not simply a matter of a person's choice. It has very much to do with a person's context. When we place all responsibility for sin on the individual it is a convenient denial of the circle of complicity that engages the larger community's choices, policies, and structures. This complicity can be traced within the family and extended to the micro- and macro-economic structures of the society. I was struck by the words of James Irwin, who has worked for twenty-six years at the Maine Youth Center. Responding to the public outcry over rising youth violence, he indicated puzzlement at the public's surprise, adding that he had

23. Dorothy Soelle, *Thinking About God* (Philadelphia: Trinity Press, 1990), pp. 77 ff.
24. From a television interview on *Sixty Minutes*, Dec. 26, 1993.

never met a murderer whose behavior couldn't be explained by his or her child-hood experiences.[25]

The same point has been made countless times before: Social as well as in-dividual factors contribute to aberrant behavior. In adopting a notion of redemp-tive grace that is purely individualized, we have inadvertently accepted its corollary assumption: that the problem of sin is individualized. And clearly, it is not. There is a circle of complicity.

The Dalai Lama, responding to a question about his anger at the 1990 Gulf War, painted a picture of this circle of complicity.

> When people started blaming Saddam Hussein, then my heart went out to him because this blaming everything on him—it's unfair. He may be a bad man, but without his army, he cannot act as aggressively as he does. And his army, without weapons, cannot do anything. And these weapons were not produced in Iraq itself. Who supplied them? Western nations! So one day something happened and they blamed everything on him—without acknowledging their own contributions. That's wrong.[26]

To think of redemption and, therefore, of sin in individualized terms per-mits us to deny our hand in the matter. Sin is a corporate, collective reality, as well as a personal one. So too is redemption. Our penal system, when it ad-dresses redemption at all, is structured as if redemption were individual and nonhistorical. And behind that is the spirit of the times. These criminals have made their bed and now they must lie in it or get out of it on their own. But to a large extent, they have not made their own bed. Their beds have been made by a far larger reality.

A recently completed study uncovered the startling fact that 75 percent of all prisoners within the New York State prison system came from seven neigh-borhoods in New York City.[27] Only denial could allow us to think that these neighborhoods are simply the gathering places for such persons, rather than the breeding grounds. To think of redemptive grace as working in the hearts of in-dividuals alone contributes to the spirit of punishment in at least two ways.

Its first contribution is *denial*. As previously mentioned, the notion of re-demptive grace denies the complexity of the causes and the needed changes at the historical, social level. Further, it contributes to a denial of our own involve-ment: The fact that our choices, our privileges, our willingness to maintain or at least not to challenge the status quo all contribute to the state of these seven

---

25. James Irwin, "The Violent Society Reaches Maine," in *The Maine Times*, Nov. 12, 1993.

26. Claudia Dreifus, "The Dali Lama," in *The New York Times* Magazine, Nov. 28, 1993, p. 54.

27. "Convicts Seek to Help Youths in Crime Areas," in *The New York Times*, Dec. 23, 1992.

neighborhoods. Whatever else such denial accomplishes, it allows us to remain self-righteous and inappropriately without guilt.

The corollary of this is that it allows us, with a clear conscience, to blame the victims. Someone must be responsible for the sorry state of affairs: for the crime, for the human degradation. This "someone" must be those whom we can target as criminals. They are the guilty ones and our vengeance is an appropriate response to their guilt. In a very real way, vengeance can only be affirmed when we consider ourselves beyond the circle of complicity. Perhaps that is why we are told to leave vengeance to God, the only one beyond the circle of complicity.

The penal system is, for the most part, an institutional response to a collective spirit of punishment harbored by those who consider themselves beyond blame. And I suspect that this sense of blamelessness has very much to do with the assumed ontological differences mentioned above that contribute to constructing false realities above being itself. Ironically, the assumption of blame and blamelessness has little relationship to the reality. For example, in New York State prisons, over 70 to 80 percent of the prisoners are black or Latino, drawn from a few inner-city neighborhoods. The majority of those imprisoned are there for drug-related crimes. But while those imprisoned are mostly people of color, as the state commissioner of corrections acknowledges, the reality is that more Euro-Americans engage in drug abuse than blacks or Latinos.[28]

The attempt to clarify the falsification of blame does not, on the other hand, deny personal accountability on the part of those who commit crimes. It is true that we are each responsible, at least to some degree, for our decisions and actions. No crime should escape the call to accountability. But Protestantism's problem has never been in holding individuals accountable. Its problem has been the failure to understand the collective or social nature of sin and redemption. And that failure has reinforced the societal spirit of punishment being deserved by those whom Protestantism quickly and easily designates as "criminal." This analysis and critique are part of a larger work in progress, but let me here briefly indicate a different understanding of grace that I would propose as the basis for an alternative response to crime.

Grace can only be adequately understood as involving two circles: the circle of creation and the circle of redemption. The circle of creation links us inextricably with God, each other, and the universe. It implies a radical cosmic ecology in which each organism is part of the other, interdependent on one another, created in relationship to, to and a greater or lesser extent with, a responsibility for the other. Nothing is outside the pale of God's goodness and love. This sensitivity led Albert Schweitzer to refuse even to harm insects.

---

28. Ibid.

A response to crime based on a radical cosmic ecology can never consider persons as toxic waste, as "animals," as something other than brother or sister. In the very act of creation we are bound together in a circle of reciprocity. As Buber says, paraphrasing the first chapter of John's Gospel, "In the beginning is the relation."[29] Certainly it is possible for persons to take advantage of that relationship, to distort it, to twist it beyond recognition. But it is impossible to destroy it. No matter what, we are God's, we are each other's, we are the world's. No grace-full response to crime can ignore this bottom line. The almost totally adversarial nature of our legal and penal systems belies this truth. Almost every step of the process sets the accused over against the society. At their best, Israel and the early church offer us a different way to understand the offender. In both these communities, one of the traditions of justice making began with the recognition of God's covenant relationship with the people and that the offender is a child of the covenant, a member of the household, a son or daughter—even when prodigal.

It is naive to think we can eliminate the anger or rage engendered by criminal offenses. But there can be more than anger and rage. There can also be deep sadness for the brother or sister, the loved one who has lost the way. Only when our criminal-justice system is based on the circle of creation rather than on the categorization of "other" can we hope to substitute justice for punishment.

The second circle of grace is the circle of redemption. Like the circle of creation that involves a cosmic ecology, the circle of redemption is also all-encompassing. True redemption must involve several aspects. The first aspect is the recognition on the part of the offender that he or she is responsible for the act committed, the choices made, the path taken. There can be no grace-full redemption without the offender's acknowledgment and personal repentance. In this regard, our faith speaks of the need for confession. Confession in our penal system, however, is primarily used as a basis for negotiating a lesser penalty or, in many cases, has been coerced by means of threat. Authentic confession, on the other hand, is rooted neither in fear nor negotiation, but in genuine sorrow and repentance. The first step in a grace-full penal system involves a penitential process that allows for this grief and sorrow to emerge. The various aids to penitence such as the original Quaker notion of the penitentiary, of bringing the offender and the victim(s) into a sustained relationship, bear serious reconsideration. At the very least, confession born of punishment is untrustworthy.

The second aspect of the circle of redemption is the recognition that the broader society is complicitous in the production of criminality. Our priorities, our deafness and blindness, our desires, our behaviors, our maintenance of cer-

---

29. Martin Buber, *I and Thou*, edited by Walter Kaufman (New York: Charles Scribner's Sons, 1970), p. 69.

tain privileges—all participate in the structures of criminality. Zoning laws, taxes, investments, job availability, educational resources—all these relate to the shaping of neighborhoods that breed crime. There is a correlation between one group's disproportionate privileges and opportunities and another group's disproportionate lack of privileges and opportunities. No one is blameless.

The third aspect of the circle of redemption involves restitution to those who have been harmed or diminished, to the extent that such restitution is possible. The economic costs born by the victims of crime in our society generally go uncompensated, in large measure because of the way in which we treat the offender. It is impossible for prisoners to make financial restitution when they are restricted to making license plates or working on chain gangs for fifty cents an hour. Until they are provided with some legitimate vehicle by which they can "pay back" the victims of their crime, the circle is incomplete. Often, of course, the restitution cannot be limited to money. The harm done may be much more profound, involving loss of relationships, loss of possibilities, loss of self-esteem. "Payback" in these cases is far more complicated and will probably entail a continuing face-to-face relationship between the offender and the offended, often with third-party help. Churches, mosques, and synagogues can become "safe spaces" for such rebuilding and could provide resources for facilitating this very difficult process.

The fourth aspect of the circle of redemption involves what most people think of when they hear the word *rehabilitation*, namely, the opportunity to develop skills and knowledge that will make the prisoner a potentially productive member of the society upon release. Lamentably, most states are cutting back on whatever it takes to provide such rehabilitative opportunities.

Finally, the circle is not complete until the offender becomes fully integrated back into the larger community of work, worship, love, and friendship. To release people from incarceration with forty dollars in their pocket and tell them to go into the world and make good is cynical at best and criminal at worst. There needs to be a community prepared to hold them to their bosom, to welcome them with the fatted calf, to rejoice that "my child who was lost, is now found."

There are not easy answers to what has become one of the most frightening societal problems. These few clues are only a small step in the right direction, but they are offered as part of a dialogue that is able to move us beyond punishment and into the authentic grace of a loving God.

Questions for Thought and Discussion

1. Discuss why and how there is such a disproportionate number of racial-ethnic people trapped in the U.S. penal system.

2. Describe your feelings about a pioneering education program for long-term prisoners being run by a theological institution.

3. Discuss the statement "Criminals deserve to be made to suffer in proportion to the suffering they have inflicted on others."

4. Discuss the crime situation in the community where you live and work. What can churches do?

5. Discuss the statement "Class and racial interests have turned prisons into the warehouses for the unwanted and increasingly unneeded underclass of our society." Do you agree or disagree? Why?

6. Is it possible to offer restitution to those who have been harmed or diminished? Why or why not?

3 | The Vocation of a Theologian
James H. Cone

No one has made a greater contribution to the study of black religion in the second half of the twentieth century than Gayraud S. Wilmore, one of the most influential and creative black activists, Christian ethicists, historians, and theologians of our time. A man of genuine humility, endowed with profound religious insight, I can say without the slightest reservation that Gayraud has influenced my thinking about black religion and theology more than any other scholar in the black freedom movement. No one is more deserving than he—as a leader in the Presbyterian Church, in the African American community, and in the black theology movement—to be recognized by this book. I only regret that the ecumenical black church—the Baptists, the Methodists, the Catholics, the Pentecostals, and all the others—*together* did not sponsor the event honoring him at the 1995 annual meeting of the National Black Presbyterian Caucus in Memphis, Tennessee. Gayraud has been a leader not just among black Presbyterians, but also in the black religious community in the United States and around the world.

What captivated me most about Gayraud's intellectual work was his deep love for black people—our origins in Africa, our determined resistance against slavery and segregation, and our fighting spirituality. The spiritual power of black resistance, he reminded us, was derived from Africa and fused with Western Christianity, but was not exhausted by either. When the history of black religion and theology in the United States is written for the second half of the twentieth century, Gayraud's great contribution to the church and its theology will occupy a central place in the story.

I do not say this to flatter Gayraud, his wife Lee, or his many friends. I say it because I am convinced of the truth of it. I am usually too blunt in my critical evaluation of black and white theologians and seldom, if ever, engage in excessive praise that is so typical in the black church, especially for occasions celebrating persons. I have never liked empty praise. Speak the truth or do no speak at all. I have been deeply challenged and spiritually fed by Gayraud's life and work. I could not say no to the invitation to contribute to this volume, because Gayraud's life and work are theological treasures, great gifts to the black church that it ignores at its own peril. Unfortunately, the black church too often ignores its theologians and scholars and heaps excessive praise on its preachers. But what would the Christian tradition have been without profound thinkers like Paul and Augustine, John Calvin and Martin Luther, Reinhold Niebuhr and Martin Luther King Jr.? A similar profundity is found in the thought of Gayraud Wilmore. His creative insights into the historical and theological meaning of black religion and theology in the United States is rivaled only by the most influential black intellectual in America's history—the great W. E. B. DuBois.

I first met Gayraud Wilmore nearly thirty years ago. We immediately became friends and since then we have traveled around the world together, advancing the cause of black theology. We have written articles and books as joint authors, a symbol of both our mutual respect and our enduring friendship. But friendship and intellectual respect have not lessened the passion of our public and private debates about the meaning of black religion and theology. I have been deeply moved by Gayraud's ministry and I value his work as being an indispensable contribution to an understanding of the faith of the black community.

My association with Gayraud reinforced in my spiritual and intellectual consciousness what it means to be a black Christian theologian. He reminded me that black theology is not white theology painted black. Black theology must be derived from and based in the black community—both inside and outside the denominational black churches. Wilmore's spiritual wisdom and challenging theological critique forced me to rethink much of what I wrote in *Black Theology and Black Power* (1969) and *A Black Theology of Liberation* (1970). He put the issue rhetorically: "Is black theology simply the Blackenization of the whole spectrum of traditional Christian theology, with particular emphasis upon the liberation of the oppressed, or does it find in the experience of oppression of black people, as black, a singular religiosity, identified not only with Christianity, but with other religions as well?!" Referring specifically to a statement I made in my first book, he continued, building on his rhetorical question: "To say that being black in America has little to do with skin color is, at best, only half true. It is possible to argue that in a world dominated by white power that has been inextricable from white Christianity, being black . . . is a unique experience and has produced a unique religion, closely related to, but not exclusively bound by, the Christian tradition."

I have been wrestling with the truth of that insight since it first was articulated in my presence, which happened more often than I cared to hear it. But I needed to ponder the meaning of those words before their meaning could be truly assimilated into my intellectual consciousness. I know, however, that I have never satisfied Gayraud Wilmore on this theological point. Nevertheless, I have endeavored to listen carefully to this telling critique of my theological program. I have been obliged to revisit my theological education, to evaluate it more critically in the light of sources and perspectives in the black experience. What, then, does it mean to do Christian theology using *black* sources rather than European theological ideas and people at the starting point?

Doing Christian theology is a task that arises from one's commitment to Jesus Christ in the context of a community of faithful people who are searching for an understanding of God's meaning for their lives in the world today. The urge to do Christian theology does not arise primarily from intellectual curiosity, though theology is not anti-intellectual. The motivation for theological reflection is like the motivation to preach the gospel. They both arise from faith itself. In preaching, one experiences the urgency to proclaim, to tell the world about what God has done in Jesus Christ to set the captives free. In theology, one experiences the urgency to *understand*, to reflect on what the gospel means in a world that is everchanging, complex, and oppressive. Without the spirit-filled proclamation of the gospel, there can be no genuine celebration of the good news of salvation—the hope that what is wrong will be put right. Without critical theological reflection, there is no way to know whether our liturgical celebrations bear witness to the one who defines the heart of the gospel, Jesus Christ. Theology, then, is faith demanding that it be understood, that we know the content of the gospel that we preach and that we know why we preach it.

To clarify my theological vocation, I often reflect back on my early years in Bearden, Arkansas—a rural community of approximately twelve hundred people. I do not remember Bearden for nostalgic reasons. In fact, I seldom return there in person, because of persistent racial tensions in my relations to the whites and lingering ambivalence in my feelings toward the blacks. I am not and do not wish to be Bearden's favorite son. My brother, Cecil, also a theologian and a preacher, has had that honor bestowed on him by the black community, a distinction he gladly accepts and a role he fulfills quite well.

I remember Bearden because it is the place where I first discovered myself and, to borrow the prophet Isaiah's language, where "I saw also the Lord" (Isa. 6:1, KJV). At Macedonia A.M.E. Church every Sunday and sometimes on weeknights, I encountered Jesus through arousing sermons, fervent prayers, spiritual songs, and the passionate testimonies of the people. Jesus was the dominant reality at Macedonia and the black life in Bearden. The people walked with him and told him about their troubles as if he were a trusted friend who understood their trials and tribulations in this unfriendly world. They sang Joseph Scriven's "What a Friend We Have in Jesus," Charles A. Tindley's "Leave It There," and Johnson Oatman, Jr.'s "No, Not One!" with heartfelt conviction and passion. They urged one another to "never be discouraged" because "there's not a friend like the lowly Jesus" who "knows our every weakness." "Take your burden to the Lord and leave it there." They called him a "way-maker," a "heart-fixer" and a "mind-regulator." They also said that Jesus was "the lily of the valley and the bright and morning star," a "wheel in the middle of a wheel," the Rose of Sharon and the Lord of life," a "very present help in the time of trouble."

The people often shouted and danced, clapped their hands and stamped their feet as they proclaimed in song, sermon, and prayer the power of Jesus' presence in their midst—"building them up where they are torn down and propping them up on every leaning side."

Jesus became a significant presence in my life too. I do not remember the exact date or time I "turned to Jesus," as the conversion experience was called, and decided to follow the Christian way. At home, church, and school, at play and at work, Jesus was always there, like an anchor in my life, giving it meaning and purpose and bestowing hope and faith in the ultimate justice of things. Like the people of Macedonia, I regarded Jesus as a confidant and savior, the one who gave me the strength and courage to be black in a society defined by white supremacy. He protected me from the sickness of hate and filled me with a self-love that empowered me to know I was not the worthless human being that white people said I was.

There were no atheists in "Cotton Belt," as the "colored" section of Bearden was called—no proclaimers of Nietzsche's "God is dead" philosophy and none of the "cultured despisers of religion" to whom Friedreich Schleiermacher addressed his work in 1799. The closest to Nietzsche's atheists and Schleiermacher's "cultured despisers" were the bluespeople who drank corn whiskey and boogied slowly and sensually to the deep guttural sounds of the raunchy, raw, gutbucket music at the juke joints every Friday and Saturday nights. The sounds of Muddy Waters, John Lee Hooker, T-Bone Walker, and Howlin' Wolf took center stage as they grunted, groaned, and moaned such tunes as "Hoochie Coochie Man," "Boom, Boom, Boom," "Cold Cold Feeling," and "Somebody in My Home." Such music was called the "down-home blues" and the "low-down dirty blues."

Unlike the church people, the bluespeople found the Sunday religion of Jesus inadequate for coping with their personal problems and the social contradictions they experienced during the week. As church people soothed their souls with the song "Lord, I Want to Be a Christian," the people at the honky-tonk, the bawdy houses, transcended their agony by facing it with stoic defiance or, as James Baldwin called it, "ironic tenacity": "I got the blues, but I'm too damned mean to cry."

My mother would not allow her sons to go to the honky-tonk. Not only was it the place Christians were instructed to avoid; it was also too dangerous. A person could get stabbed, shot, and even killed in the honky-tonk. The bluespeople partied hard and late into the night. Too much booze could cause a man to lose control of his senses and thereby make the mistake of insulting another man's lady friend, mother, sister, or wife. That would cause a retaliation that was sure to draw some blood. Violence was a frequent occurrence on Friday and Saturday nights as black men sought to assert the masculinity that had been taken from them by whites during the week.

Sometimes sharp tensions emerged between the celebrants of Saturday night and those of Sunday morning. But each group respected the other, because both knew they were seeking, in their own way, to cope with the same troubles of life. Some people moved between the two groups during different periods of their lives, as my father did. But it was not possible to be a member in good standing of both groups at the same time, because the church demanded that an individual make a choice between the blues and the spirituals, between the "devil's music" and the "sweet melodies of Jesus." Baptist and Methodist churches, the only black denominations in Bearden, regularly accepted back-sliders back into the fold, provided they repented of their wrongdoing and declared their intentions to lead a good and righteous life in service to the Lord. My father had a few lapses in faith, because he found it hard to cope with life's adversities without taking a nip and hanging out with the bluespeople in order to add a little spice to life not found at the church. But my mother monitored him closely, and Macedonia readily received him back into the community of the faithful as often as he publicly repented.

What puzzled me most about the religion of Jesus during my childhood was not the tensions between Saturday night and Sunday morning in black life, but rather the conspicuous presence of the color bar in the Lord's house. In Bearden, like the rest of America, Sunday was the most segregated day of the week, and 11:00 a.m., the most segregated hour. Black and white Christians virtually had no social or religious dealings with each other, even though both were Baptists and Methodists—reading the same Bible, worshiping the same God, and reciting the same confessions of faith in the churches. The only churchly contact between blacks and whites was when one or two of the so-called "good whites" would accept an invitation to attend one of the black churches. The whites who came were set apart for special recognition for their service to the black community. But such social occasions were rare, because whites did not want to give blacks the impression that the two communities were equal in any way—not in the society, nor in the house of the Lord. While the prominently posted "Welcome" signs outside white churches ostensibly beckoned all visitors to join them in worship, blacks knew that the invitation did not include them.

"What kind of Christianity is it that preaches love and practices segregation?" my brother Cecil and I, budding young theologians, often asked each other. "How could whites exclude black people from their churches and still claim Jesus as their Savior and the Bible as their holy book?" We talked about testing the theological integrity of white faith by seeking to integrate one of their churches, but later decided that the risks of bodily harm were too great.

I had a happy childhood, surrounded by a loving mother and father, a caring black community, many friends, and two older brothers who allowed me to exercise a power and an influence in our relationship that my physical size and intelligence did not warrant. I do not remember ever having my humanity crushed. To be sure, I grew up during the age of Jim Crow (the 1940s and early 1950s). I attended segregated schools, drank water from "colored" fountains, went to movies in balconies, and when necessary greeted white adults at the back door of their homes. I also observed the contempt and brutality that white law meted out to blacks who transgressed to racial mores or who dared to question their authority. Bearden white people, like most white Southerners, could be mean and vicious, and I, along with other blacks, avoided them whenever possible—as though they were poisonous snakes.

But in spite of the ugly behavior of whites and the dehumanizing rules they enforced on blacks, I had a wonderful childhood and did not grow up with fear or hatred toward anyone—white or black. The reason has mainly to do with my faith in Jesus, mediated through the spirituality of the black Christians of Macedonia and the other black churches of Bearden. Because of this faith, I have always known that my worth as a human being was not determined by what others said about me but rather by what God said and did in the moment of creation and in the redemptive act of Jesus Christ.

Grounded in this faith, it did not matter what whites said about me, because I knew that "I am somebody"—a child of God created for freedom and for a special ministry in the church and the world. Racial obscenities, like "nigger," "coon," and "spook," so typical of Southern whites during my childhood, went in one ear and out the other. I sometimes hurled racial epithets, like "white trash" and "rednecks," right back at them. But more frequently I merely laughed at them to myself and with other blacks, and even pitied them, because I soon realized, as James Baldwin said, "Whoever debases others is debasing himself." I do not ever remember experiencing a feeling of inferiority in the presence of whites because of what they said about me or about other black people. One reason was the stellar example my father and mother set for me. They were a part of that cloud of black witnesses that Baldwin wrote about who "in the teeth of the most terrible odds achieved an unassailable and monumental dignity." They taught me what Baldwin told his nephew: "You can only be destroyed by believing that you really are what the white world calls a *nigger*."

My parents were not niggers. They were strong and self-confident, exhibiting a determined opposition to white supremacy, creative leadership, and great courage when they and the black community faced adversity. Charlie and Lucy, as the people in Bearden called them, were immensely intelligent, even though they had little opportunity for formal education, having completed only the sixth and ninth grades, respectively. With the support and encouragement of my father, my mother went back and completed high school where her sons had graduated earlier. She also went on to finish her college degree four years later and then returned to teach in Bearden. I was struck by her determination. Their education, they often told their sons, came from the "school of hard knocks"—

the experience of surviving with dignity in a society that did not recognize black humanity. The lives of my parents, along with other poor blacks, past and present, convinced me that the most likely candidates for a less than human status were not the victims of injustice, but rather the people most responsible for oppressing them.

Fortunately, the faith of Macedonia did not allow for the distinction of superior and inferior races. "Out of one blood," I was taught at home and Sunday school, "God created everyone—blacks, whites, and other races; men, women, and children." No person or group is better than any other. As evidence for that claim, preachers often cited text from the prophet Malachi: "Have we not all one father? Hath not one God created us?" (2:10, KJV). They also quoted Paul selectively—carefully avoiding the ambiguous and problematic texts, especially in Philemon where Paul returned the slave Onesimus to his master, and in Ephesians where servants were told to "be obedient to them who are your masters . . . as unto Christ" (Eph. 6:5, KJV).

Preachers and Sunday school teachers at Macedonia were quite skilled in picking biblical texts that affirmed their humanity. They often quoted Paul's letter to the church at Galatia, especially the part where he writes: "There is neither Jew nor Greek . . . neither slave nor free . . . neither male nor female." We are "all one in Christ Jesus" (see Gal. 3:28, KJV)—blacks and whites, as well as other human colors and characteristics. When we believe that gospel and internalize it in our way of life, as many black Christians in Bearden did, it transforms us, causing us to love ourselves and others and enabling us to do and speak the truth with a power and clarity not derived exclusively from human initiative.

From the time I was conscious of being a Christian, I knew I had to communicate the gospel to the world. The gospel is not something that can be kept to oneself. It must be shared with the brokenhearted and downtrodden, the "lowly down under," as the great folklorist Zora Neal Hurston called them. Since preaching was the dominant mode of communicating the gospel in the black community, I decided at the early age of sixteen to enter the ministry, a vocation I initially identified exclusively with pastors of churches and traveling evangelists. But even at that time, I did not feel comfortable with everything I heard and saw happening in the churches among black preachers and other church leaders. They not only seemed to tolerate anti-intellectualism as whites tolerated racism, but they, like whites in relation to racism, often promoted it. It was as if the less one knew and the louder one shouted Jesus' name, the closer one was to God.

I found it hard to believe that the God of Jesus, who was regarded by the people as almighty and all-knowing, condoned ignorance as if it were a virtue. It contradicted what my parents and teachers taught me about the value of education and a disciplined mind. It also contradicted what I read in history books about black slaves who risked life and limb in order to learn how to read and write so they could understand more clearly the meaning of the freedom to which God had called them. I was, therefore, deeply troubled by the anti-intellectualism that permeated many aspects of the ministry in the black church.

As I explored the range of human knowledge in the sciences, literature, history, and philosophy at Shorter and Philander Smith colleges, my concern for the need of an educated, learned ministry was intensified. For me, religion and education were tied together. Together they liberated the mind and spirit from the fetters of ignorance and immorality. They also empowered people to take charge of their lives, to take hold of history and create a liberating future. I was determined to get as much religion and education as possible.

How could ministers preach a relevant and liberating gospel in a world they did not understand? How can they understand the gospel without careful study, critical debate, and disciplined reflection? W. E. B. DuBois said that a religion that won't stand the application of reason and common sense is not fit for an intelligent dog. Meeting a few seminary and university trained A.M.E. and Baptist ministers who encouraged *critical* thinking and discussion about the nature and function of the church reinforced my conviction in the value of education. Thereby, I was helped to sustain my belief that the church could not remain faithful to its God apart from continuous, prophetic criticism of what it says and does in Jesus' name.

Although I was the pastor of two small A.M.E. churches during my college years and had planned to return to that ministry following three years of seminary education, I knew when I first chose the ministry as my vocation that I had to understand the meaning of the gospel I had been entrusted to proclaim. How could I preach what I did not understand? The search for a comprehensive and coherent understanding of the gospel in a complex and changing world was the chief motivation that led me to study at Garrett Biblical Institute (now Garrett-Evangelical Theological Seminary). It seemed that the more I learned about the gospel through a critical study of the Bible, history, theology, and the practice of ministry, the more I needed and wanted to know about it. I wanted to explore its meanings for different social, political, and cultural contexts, past and present.

Theology quickly became my favorite subject in seminary because it opened the door to explore the meaning of the Christian faith for the current time and situation in which I was living. I loved the give and take of theological debate and eagerly waited for the opportunity during and after class to engage my professors and fellow students on a particular theological issue. That was why I remained at Garrett and Northwestern University for the Ph.D. in systematic theology. After I completed the doctorate in the fall of 1964, writing a dissertation of Karl Barth's anthropology, I thought I had enough knowledge of the Christian faith to communicate it to persons anywhere in the world. Who would not feel adequately endowed after reading twelve volumes of Barth's *Church Dogmatics*?

But black students at Philander Smith College in Little Rock, Arkansas (my first teaching post), and the Civil Rights and Black Power movements of the 1960s awakened me from my theological slumber. As I became actively involved in the black freedom movement that was happening in the streets all over America, I soon discovered how limited my seminary education had been. The curriculum at both Garrett and Northwestern had not dealt with questions that black people were asking as they searched for the theological meaning of their fight for justice in a white racist society. And as individuals and isolated students within a demanding educational system, neither I nor the token number of black students had the intellectual resources to articulate them. I found myself grossly ill-prepared, because I knew deep down that I could not repeat to a struggling black community the doctrines of the faith as they had been reinterpreted by Barth, Bultmann, Niebuhr, and Tillich for European colonizers and white racists in the United States. I knew before I could say anything worthwhile about God and black oppression in the United States, I had to discover a theological identity that was accountable to the life, history, and culture of African American people.

In a way, my education had pulled me away from my people. The education quest had been to master the theological systems of the well-known European theologians of the past and present. As students, we obediently spent most of our time reading books, listening to lectures, and writing papers about their views of God, Jesus, the Holy Spirit, and the church. But because I recognized the community to whom I was accountable, I wanted to know more than just what Europeans and white Americans who emulated them thought about sacred reality. I was searching for a way to create a Christian theology out of the black experience of slavery, segregation, and the struggle for a just society.

When I asked my professors about what theology had to do with the black struggle for racial justice, they seemed surprised and uncomfortable with the question, not knowing what to say and anxious to move on with the subject matter as they understood it. I was often told that theology and the struggle for racial justice were separate subjects, with the latter belonging properly to the disciplines of sociology and political science. Although I felt a disquieting unease with the response, I did not say much about it to my professors as they skirted around what the gospel had to say to black people in a white society that had defined them as nonpersons.

When I got out of seminary and graduate school, the blackness in my theological consciousness exploded like a volcano after many dormant years. I found my theological voice. Using the cultural and political insights of Malcolm X and Martin Luther King Jr., I discovered a way of articulating what I wanted to say about theology and race that not only rejected the need for my professors' approval, but challenged them to exorcise the racism in their theologies. Malcolm taught me how to make theology black and never again to despise my African origin. Martin showed me how to make and keep theology Christian. I was transformed from a *Negro* theologian to a black theologian, from an understanding of theology as an analysis of God-ideas in books, to an understanding of it as disciplined reflection about God that arose from a commitment to the political practice of justice for the poor.

The turn to blackness was an even deeper *metanoia*-experience than the turn to Jesus. It was spiritual, transforming radically my way of seeing the world and theology. Before I was born again into thinking black, I thought of theology as something remote from my history and culture, something that was primarily defined by Europeans that I, at best, could only imitate. Blackness gave me new theological spectacles that enabled me to move beyond the limits of white theology and empowered my mind to think thoughts that were considered wild, heretical when evaluated by white standards. Blackness opened my eyes to see black history and culture as the most insightful source for knowing about God outside of the Bible. Blackness whetted my appetite for learning how to do theology with a black signature on it and, thereby, make it accountable to poor black people and not to the privileged white theological establishment. The revolution that Malcolm X created in my theological consciousness meant that I could no longer make peace with the intellectual mediocrity in which I had been trained. The more I trusted my experience, the more new thoughts about God and theology whirled around in my brain—so fast I could hardly contain my excitement.

Using the black experience as the starting point of theology raised the theodicy question in a profound and challenging way that was never mentioned in graduate school. It was James Baldwin who poignantly defined the problem for me when he said that, if God's love was so great, and if God loved all God's children, why were we, the blacks, cast down so far? This was an existential, heart-wrenching question that upset everything I had learned in graduate school about the problem of evil. It forced me to delve deeper into a wellspring of blackness, not for an answer, but for a way of doing theology that liberated it from the dominant culture of Europe and North America.

In writing *Black Theology and Black Power* (1969) and *A Black Theology of Liberation* (1970), I suddenly understood what Karl Barth must have felt when he first rejected the liberal theology of his professors in Germany. It was a liberating experience to be free of my neo-orthodox professors, to be emancipated from the habit of defining theology with abstract theological jargon that was unrelated to the life-and-death issues of race. Although separated from him by nearly fifty years, and dealing with completely different theological situations and issues, I felt a spiritual kinship with Barth, especially his *The Epistle to the Romans* (1921) and his public debate with Adolf Harnack, his former teacher.

As I think back to that time in the late 1960s, when white American theologians were writing and talking about the "death of God theology" while black people were fighting and dying in the streets, the energy swells once again. I was angry and could not keep it to myself. Like Malcolm, I felt I was the angriest black theologian in America. I had to speak out against the hypocrisy I witnessed in theology, the churches, and society. And that was why I began to write.

Being a Christian theologian is difficult in an educational environment where tenure and academic security are highlighted as the chief goals. In fact, the things theologians are called on to say are almost guaranteed to preclude such rewards. For a theologian to write in order to gain great professional esteem and status is to miss one's calling—to misinterpret one's vocation to be a truth-teller about the human condition of injustice. In writing to gain academic acceptance, one may very well be giving tacit support to the status quo and hence to the injustices it perpetuates. Theological writing should come out of the spiritual depths of political struggle and should be motivated and sustained by a need to understand the faith in a racially-torn, poverty-stricken, gender-biased, and class-oriented global society and church. Theologians should be searching for the truth in the revolutionary activity of poor people's struggle for justice. We should be searching for the truth that Jesus promised shall set people free.

I did not begin to write about a black theology of liberation because I hate white people, or even because I enjoy exposing the hypocrisy of white Christianity. I do not hate anybody, because, as Baldwin said, it is "too heavy a sack to carry." I, therefore, receive absolutely no delight in scolding white theologians about the racism in their theology, or in pointing out how inhumane and brutal white Christians have been in their behavior toward blacks. My only concern is to speak what Malcolm called the "naked, undiluted truth" as clearly and as forcefully as I know how, in an effort to fulfill my vocation as a theologian of the church, where I am called to bear witness to God's liberating presence in the world. There is no way to speak the truth and do the will of God in an oppressive society without offending those who are responsible for the oppression or who identify with the enemies of justice.

Nor do I write about a black theology of liberation because I like criticizing the leadership of African American churches. I love the black church and am considered one of its leaders. But as Martin King said, "There comes a time when silence is betrayal." King was referring to America's war in Vietnam, but his statement is applicable to other times and situations of injustice. It is especially relevant today when both black and white people, and their churches, often separate spirituality from the struggle for justice. I cannot sit by in silence as I watch black ministers defile the church of Richard Allen, Sojourner Truth, Jarena Lee, Fannie Lou Hamer, and Martin Luther King Jr. Black church leaders should ponder what the prophet Amos said to the religious people of his time: "I hate, I despise your festivals and I take no delight in your solemn assemblies. . . . Take away from me the noise of your songs; I will not listen to the melody of your harps. But let justice roll down like waters, and righteousness like an everflowing stream" (Amos 5:21, 23–24).

This text was one of Martin King's favorites, and he repeated it often to apathetic blacks and complacent whites who seemed not to recognize that Christians cannot retain their identity without being actively involved in the fight for racial justice. When King saw large, expensive white church buildings in Mississippi, with their towering steeples, in the midst of the extreme poverty of black poor, he asked: "Who worships in those buildings? Who is their God?" When I see a similar loathsome phenomenon in the black community today (five- and six million-dollar church structures and preachers seemingly more interested in personal gain and status than the well-being of the poor), I too must ask: "Who is their God?" Who is our God? That is the central theological question for me.

As theologians analyze the identity of the gospel that the church preaches, they should also examine their own conscience daily and scrutinize their motivation for studying and writing theology and ethics. Is it because we are concerned about personal gain or status? Are we seeking acceptance in an academic community that is largely unconcerned about justice and the well-being of the poor? If that is the primary reason, then we need to be delivered from ourselves, from the ever-present danger of thinking of ourselves more highly than we ought. Of course, it is easy to deceive ourselves on matters like this. Humility itself can become a form of pride. "Lord, look at us, we are not seeking personal gain." God forbid that we become so humble that our humility becomes distorted into a form of pride.

While acknowledging that we must be careful to watch out for false humility, authentic humility is good for the soul and also for the development of one's vocation as a theological scholar. If we seek to become scholars of and for the church of Jesus Christ, then status and personal gain should become secondary to our primary aim of doing and telling the truth. Success as theologians and students of theology should be secondary to the goal of loving God and neighbor and taking sides in the political struggles of the weak and helpless against the rich and the powerful. We should remember always what Jesus said: "For those who want to save their life will lose it, and those who lose their life for my sake, and for the sake of the gospel, will save it" (Mark 8:35). This saying is just as true today as it was when Jesus said it, and it is as true for us as ministers, professors, and students of theology as it is for janitors, maids, and secretaries.

No one understood this theological truth more profoundly than Martin Luther King Jr. In a well-known sermon titled "The Drum Major Instinct," delivered at Atlanta's Ebenezer Baptist Church where he was co-pastor with his father, two months before his assassination, King acknowledged the desire in everyone "to be important, to surpass others, to achieve distinction, to lead the parade" as a drum major. He did not deny that feeling in himself—that sense of wanting to be first, just as James and John demonstrated when they asked Jesus to allow them to sit, one on the right, and the other on the left, in his glory. But King remembered what Jesus said to the sons of Zebedee and to the other disciples who resented their request. "Whoever wishes to be first among you must be slave of all" (Mark 10:44). The only way to be great and important in Jesus' world is to be the servant of the least. That was why King said he wanted to be a drum major for truth, peace, and justice.

As theologians, whether professional or lay, we should follow King's example. We should teach and write because we have been called to be the servants of the truth, determined to make it so plain to human understanding that no one can preach the gospel of Jesus Christ without being judged by it. Theologians are called to be seekers after the truth, and when we discover it we must, as the slaves said in their spiritual song, "Go tell it on the mountain, over the hills and everywhere." The truth, as the prophet Jeremiah said, is like "a burning fire shut up in my bones; I am weary with holding it in, and I cannot" (Jer. 20:9). We must tell the truth with all the intellectual passion and power God has given to us. Only then can we fulfill our theological vocation.

Questions for Thought and Discussion

1. Discuss the statement "The black church too often ignores its theologians/scholars and heaps excessive praise on its preachers." Is this an accurate statement? Why or why not?

2. Discuss the statement "Black theology is not white theology painted black." How has the church addressed this issue?

3. Was yours a conversion experience when you decided to follow the Christian way? How has this conversion made a difference in your life?

4. Were there places in your experience of growing up that your parents instructed you as a Christian to avoid? Should Christians avoid certain places?

5. Have you experienced tension as it relates to "color" in a service of worship? Describe the experience.

6. What does the gospel say to black people in a white society?

7. What is "naked, undiluted truth"? Are there examples you can describe as a Christian?

4 | Re/Membering African American Peoplehood—Resisting Its Dis/Memberment

Delores S. Williams

THE AFRICAN AMERICAN population of the United States is often referred to as a "peoplehood." An African American peoplehood is a human collective bonded by a common sociohistorical/economic experience and a cultural heritage that are held together by a furious struggle for survival, liberation, and a productive quality of life. Building on this definition, my hypothesis is straightforward. I claim that for the four hundred years the African Americans have been in the United States, their peoplehood has been under attack by the dominant sociopolitical/economic systems that organize life in this country. African American peoplehood faces the constant threat of dis/memberment by these systems. *Dis/membering* is to tear apart, to fragment and disconnect a people from their cultural roots, heritage, identity, and those resources that contribute to the strength, solidarity, and well-being of the group. During these four hundred years of attack, however, African American men and women have created a rich history of *re/membering* (or putting back together) what hostile forces have *dis/membered* or sought to dis/member by fragmenting. Professor Gayraud Wilmore stands in this long tradition of re/membering.

I tell an anecdote when I recall how Professor Wilmore's work directed my attention to this black tradition of re/membering. During the black political and cultural revolution of the 1960s, I was very active with my husband in the Civil Rights movement in Kentucky. I was annoyed by the general sluggish response of most African American churches to the struggle. Hence, I reasoned that the black church and the religion it espoused had contributed nothing to the historic freedom struggle of African American people.

During the course of the revolution, Professor Wilmore's book *Black Religion and Black Radicalism: An Interpretation of the Religious History of the Afro-American People* was published. It raised my consciousness about the African American Christian religion's great contribution to the black struggle for freedom in the United States. He introduced us young black dissidents to our people's history of resistance as it was channeled through the black church. Teaching us what schools and churches had neglected to teach, he *re/membered* or *put back together*, the story of our faith, supported by a black tradition of resistance. He gave us an understanding of our religious heritage we could respect. The education we had received in schools had *dis/membered* us from the foundations of black history as told by black people.

With Professor Wilmore's example as my guide, I support my original hypothesis in two ways. Initially I describe in this chapter what I see to be negative sociohistorical realities dis/membering or threatening to dis/member black people over time. Next I demonstrate how African Americans have re/membered their peoplehood or held it together in defiance of the threat of dis/memberment.

Hostile Forces

I identify four negative forces that have historically worked against solidarity in the African American community. One of the most cruel hostilities is white racism, which (1) denies black communities entrance into the mainstream of economic life in the United States—thus poverty becomes a chronic, physical condition often generating behavior that disconnects people from the sustenance of positive community life; (2) denies black people the quality of public education that equips them to participate in and contribute to the growth of community and nation; (3) attacks and often destroys the self-esteem and self-love necessary for holding a healthy peoplehood together; and (4) attempts to destroy the human spirit in black people by denying that they are human.

White racism tries to dis/member black American peoplehood when the work of white legal officers of the courts and juries incarcerates black men and women in large numbers disproportionate to the percentage of African Americans in the general population of the United States.

Second, male oppression of females has long been a threat to solidarity among black women and men. Unfortunately, too many men and too many black churches have, in relation to black women, subscribed to a negative ethical norm sanctioned by most cultures around the globe. That norm is female subordination to males. Womanist scholars in theology, ethics, biblical studies, and the practice of ministry have raised serious questions about the way this psychology, committed to the subordination of women, hinders the liberation work of the church and oppresses black women who seek to be ordained into Christian ministry. African American men have not realized that when they practice sexism by oppressing African American females, they bond with those white racist forces that oppress the entire black community.

Third, a tragic dis/membering of community happens when black consciousness begins to devalue, disregard, and forget the folk knowledge, stories, and mythmaking that has been passed along from generation to generation by old black ancestors. Much of this knowledge contains survival, liberation, and quality-of-life insights black people learned through the many years of living in an oppressive white society.

Coming of age in the Southern United States in the days of strict segregation, I remember the proverbs about survival that came from the old folks in my black community. For instance: "Don't let your mouth say something your head can't stand." (Meaning: If you are not prepared to take the consequence for what you say, then don't say it.) "A whistling girl and a cackling hen never come to a very good end." (Meaning: Don't let white folks see you, a woman, aggressively whistling like a man. They might wring your neck the same as they do a chicken that makes too much noise.) "Never pass up the opportunity to keep your mouth closed." (Meaning: If you come into a territory where you are the only black person in a sea of white people, listen carefully before you speak. Check out the terrain, *then* talk.)

The most serious threat, however, to the dis/memberment of African American peoplehood is genocide. Not long ago a woman in Harlem described what she called "genocide American style." She said that when you close off opportunities for black people through inadequate and inappropriate education, you render them unemployed and unemployable. When you take away their housing, they become beggars on the street. You constantly harass them through police brutality. You make sure the people in the community cannot accumulate wealth because you shut off their access to financing and to borrowing power from banks. You introduce a system of welfare that breaks up the home and devalues black fatherhood. You control the media so that black people are projected as criminals and the general public gets the idea that all black people are morally depraved. In other words, you render black people hopeless. Therefore, she concluded, the charge of genocide is not made against the State, even though the State has been one of the chief architects of black hopelessness and death.

Black Americans have not been passive to these constant attacks on their solidarity. Through the creation of life-sustaining traditions, they have re/membered what hostile sociohistorical forces tried to dis/member and sometimes succeeded in dis/membering. As I see it, some of these important black traditions are a wisdom tradition, an education tradition, traditions of biblical appropriation, and a literary tradition.

The Wisdom Tradition

As it developed among the old black ancestors (the folk), some of this tradition uses everyday life and humor to weave stories and anecdotes that instruct the community about the lack of justice for black people in a white world, about the superior intelligence of black women, and about how things came to be. *The Book of Negro Folklore*, edited by Langston Hughes and Arna Bontemps, contains some of these stories.

In order for the community to know that justice does not work for black people in America, the folk in their own language told the story of Sis Goose:

> Ole Sis Goose wus er-sailin' on de lake, and ole Br'er Fox was hid in de weeds. By um by, ole Sis Goose swum up close to der bank and ole Br'er Fox lept out an cotched her.
>
> "O yes, ole Sis Goose, I'se got yer now, you'se been er-sailing' on der lake er long time, en I'se got yer now. I'se gwine to break yer neck en pick yer bones."
>
> "Hole on der', Br'er Fox, hold on, I'se got jes' as much right to swimin' der lake as you has ter lie in der weeds. Hit's des' as much my lake es hit is yours, and we is gwine to take dis matter to der cotehouse and see if you has any right to break my neck and pick my bones."
>
> And so dey went to cote, and when dey got dere, de sheriff, he wus er fox, en de judge, he wus er fox, and der tourneys, dey wus foxes, en all der jurymen, dey was foxes, too.
>
> En dey tried ole Sis Goose, and dey 'victed her and dey 'scuted her and picked her bones.
>
> Now, my chilluns, listen to me, when all de folks in de cotehouse is foxes, and you is des' er common goose, der ain't gwine to be much jestice for you pore cullud folks.

One of the most humorous models of folk wisdom is the anecdote about "The Farmer and G.P.C.," which praises the superior intelligence and shrewdness of an African American woman. As the tale goes:

> One time dere was a man that was a farmer. One year he had a real good crop. But dis man was kinda lazy, and when it came time to gether de crop he tole de ole lady dat he could not he'p gather de crop cause he feld de Lord was callin' him to go preach. He tole her to look up on de sky, and he pointed out de letters G. P. C., which he say meant, "Go Preach Christ" and he had to go. But de ole lady she was to much fer hem.
>
> "Dose letters don' mean 'Go Preach Christ,'" she said. "Dey mean, 'Go Pick Cotton.'"

Just as important to the community as knowledge about justice and about women's intelligence was the account of how things came to be—especially how so many churches came to be. The black ancestors told the story of "The Rock":

> Christ was walkin' long one day wid all his disciples and he said, "We're goin' for a walk today. Everybody pick up a rock and come along." So everybody got their selves a nice big rock 'ceptin' Peter. He was lazy so he picked up a li'l bit of a pebble and dropped it in his side pocket and came along.
>
> Well, they walked all day long and de other 'leven disciples changed them rocks from one arm to de other, but they kept on totin' 'em. Long towards sundown they came 'long by de Sea of Galilee and Jesus tole 'em, "Well, le's fish awhile. Cast in yo' nets right here."
>
> They done like he tole 'em and caught a great big mess of fish. Then they cooked 'em and Christ said, "Now, all y'all bring up yo' rocks."

So they all brought they rocks and Christ turned 'em into bread and they all had a plenty to eat wid they fish 'ceptin' Peter. He couldn't hardly make a moufful offa de li'l bread he had and he didn't like dat a bit.

Two or three days after dat Christ went outdoors and looked up at de sky and says, "Well, we're goin' for anuther walk today. Everybody get yo' self a rock and come along."

They all picked up a rock apiece and was ready to go. All but Peter. He went and tore down half a mountain. It was so big he couldn't move it wid his hands. He had to take a pinch-bar to move it. All day long Christ walked and talked to his disciples and Peter sweated and strained wid dat rock of his'n.

Way long in de evenin' Christ went up under a great big old tree and set down and called all of his disciples around im and said, "Now everybody bring yo' rocks."

So everybody brought theirs but Peter. Peter was about a mile down de road punchin' dat half a mountain he was bringin.' So Christ waited til he got dere. He looked at de rocks dat der other 'leven disciples had, den he seen dis great big mountain dat Peter had and so he got up and walked over to it and put one foot up on it and said, "Why, Peter, dis is a fine rock you got here! It's a noble rock! And Peter, on dis rock A's gointer build my church."

Peter says, "Naw you ain't neither. You won't build no church house on dis rock. You gointer turn dis rock into bread!"

Christ knowed dat Peter meant dat thing so he turnt de hillside into bread and dat mountain is de bread he fed de five thousand wid. Den he took dem 'leven other rocks and glued em together and built his church on it. And that's how come de Christian churches is split up into so many different kinds—cause it's built on pieced-up rock.

This wisdom tradition of re/membering uses everyday community images to create stories that often function to provide a moral to counteract the negative effect of dis/membering forces and to convert biblical stories into a language and worldview compatible with the community's experience and sense of solidarity. Thus the folk gave voice to barnyard creatures in order to instruct the community about the lack of justice blacks could expect in a white world. They affirmed the intelligence of a black woman in a world that devalued black womanhood. They shaped God, Peter, and the eleven in language, events, and characters real to black people's experience and that were unifying for their community. Thus Christ neither quibbles with Peter nor scolds him when Peter's will is contrary to Christ's will. Rather, Christ honors Peter's intention that the mountain be turned into bread instead of becoming the foundation of the church.

In the imagination of the folk, the foundation of the church is pieced-up rock or unity. However, "pieced up" could not only suggest "pieced together," it could also suggest rock broken into pieces. This would indicate both collectivity and individualism: a dualism with which most African Americans struggle. I choose the "unity" meaning because the old women in the South I knew used the expression "pieced up" to refer to their process of making quilts by piecing together patches from old clothes. And quite literally, the story states that Christ glued together the pieces of rock held by the 'leven. Of course, this literal statement suggests that the old black folk believed it was not one person—that is, Peter, on whom Christ built the church—it was built on many.

The Education Tradition

None of the African American traditions of re/membering is more significant than the education tradition. This is a tradition that has, historically, stretched across all stratification in the African American community. It is a tradition that advises people to get an education, since "learning" (as the folk term "education") can provide knowledge about how to use the country's resources for the community's well-being and mobility. This tradition not only attempts to heal community fragmentation and isolation because of illiteracy. The education tradition also functions to remind the community that freedom can be gained through the accumulation of knowledge. Thus education helps the community to re/member social and political strategies that worked in the past to hasten freedom for black people. The education tradition reaches back into slavery, and many of those who heeded the advice to get an education achieved outstanding benefits for the African American community.

In the slave era, no story is more representative of this tradition than that of Milla Granson. Initially she was a slave in Kentucky, but she was sold farther south into Mississippi. When she was in Kentucky, her owners' children taught her to read and write. This was done secretly since it was a crime to teach slaves to read and write. So when Granson was sold farther south, the people who purchased her did not know that she possessed these skills. However, Granson began a midnight school among the slaves. She took in twelve at a time and taught them how to read and write. She graduated many slaves, some of whom forged passes and slipped away to freedom in Canada.

This tendency of passing education along to the community did not stop with Milla Granson. Mary McCleod Bethune is an example from the early twentieth century. An educated woman herself, Bethune started a college on a garbage dump with assets in the amount of $1.50. Today Bethune-Cookman College graduates many students and is a multimillion dollar institution. A contemporary of Bethune, Booker T. Washington founded Tuskegee Normal and Industrial Institute, which today is Tuskegee University. Perhaps the leading black educator in the late nineteenth and early twentieth century, Washington constantly reminded black people to "cast down your bucket where you are." That is to say, build economically in the geographic space you occupy. As a way of achieving this goal Washington advocated industrial education, which he believed would facilitate black people's self-help strategies toward economic prosperity.

Though the molders and followers of the education tradition of re/membering had a common concern for the freedom and well-being of the African American community, they often differed about the form education should take. For example, Washington stressed practical knowledge or industrial education that would equip black people with knowledge of trades and, therefore, prepare them for employment in the industries of America. W. E. B. DuBois, on the other hand, told black people to hitch their wagon to a star. He was telling them to aim as high as they could in order to develop their talents and use them to help integrate the community into the dominant society. Thus DuBois emphasized liberal arts and the classics as the way by which blacks should be educated. He thought that Washington at Tuskegee was preparing people in obsolete trades that would not be very marketable in the approaching twentieth century.

In the late twentieth century, Professor Gayraud Wilmore stands firmly in this education tradition. His special gift to the African American community has been to awaken it to the historic role black religion has played, but not only in the freedom struggle of the community. Black religion and the black church have played a major role in the formation of educational institutions for black people in the United States. Wilmore has helped the community re/member its past so that it can have a firm faith in its ability to design a supportive and productive future for itself. He models the kind of African American scholar whose work shows commitment to the highest caliber of scholarship while it maintains its accountability to the African American community and to the church.

While a wisdom tradition and an education tradition have provided vital resources for supporting the solidarity of the community with regard to survival, liberation, and a productive quality of life, the community's traditions of biblical appropriation have furnished the hope undergirding the community's faith "that trouble don't last always." This hope helps prevent total dissolution of the community.

Traditions of Biblical Appropriation

Through these traditions, black Americans have, for hundreds of years, appropriated biblical characters and situations that show God's concern for people in the same plight in which the black community found itself. The deposits of African American culture demonstrate this. For example, the spiritual songs, some slave narratives, and African-American literature in general contain many references to the biblical Moses helping God to liberate the Hebrew people from oppression in Egypt. Many black parents have named their children Moses. In fact, the great black nineteenth-century female liberator, Harriet Tubman, who liberated many African American slaves, was called "the Moses of her people." Daniel was delivered from the lion's den'; the Hebrew boys—Shadrach, Meshach, and Abednego—were delivered from a fiery furnace; Paul and Silas were delivered from jail. All these biblical figures appear in the songs and stories of the black community to show God's liberating power. In my work, I refer to this as the liberation tradition of African American biblical appropriation.

There is another tradition of African American biblical appropriation. It is the survival/quality-of-life tradition that is presently being explored in the scholarship of some African American womanist theologians. It focuses on the biblical figure of Hagar whom African Americans have appropriated for over one hundred years. The plight of Hagar has been represented in the fine arts and repeated in slave narratives, poetry, novels, and short stories of black Americans—especially in the work of black women.

In my own book *Sisters in the Wilderness: The Challenge of Womanist God-Talk*, I explore this African American appropriation of Hagar in order to discern why black people have so widely recognized and applied her story to themselves. I arrive at three basic conclusions:

The first reason for the appropriation is that Hagar's story, contained in the book of Genesis, is not only congruent with black women's history during slavery and beyond, but corresponds with aspects of the history of the entire black American community. For instance, Hagar, African American women, and the black American community have roots in Africa. They were all enslaved by non-African, foreign powers. Like black women and the black community, Hagar was at the mercy of a dominant and dominating foreign culture. She was powerless. She did not even have power over her own body. She could be brutalized whenever her owners chose to brutalize her. Thus, Sara's brutalization of Hagar is not unfamiliar to black women and the black community, for both have suffered brutalization from male and female bosses who have supervised and continue to supervise the labor force in America.

Many black women tell of the brutal treatment they have received as domestic workers in the homes of white women. Like Hagar, black women and all other black people were turned out of bondage without the economic resources needed for survival and for a productive quality of life. After she was cast out of the household of Abraham and Sarah, Hagar tried to reconnect with her African heritage by choosing a wife for her son from among her own African people. Similarly, African American women and men are attempting to reconnect with their African heritage.

A second reason why the African American community has appropriated Hagar and her story is because this story responds to the urgency of black people's need for survival resources. It corresponds to black people's—particularly black women's—faith about God's activity in their survival struggle. In Genesis 21, Hagar has been cast out of Abraham's house with her child, and she does not have enough resources for the survival of her family—herself and child. They have run out of water in the wilderness of Beersheba. Hagar weeps because she does not want her child to die. Then God provides Hagar with a survival resource. He gives her new vision to see survival resources where she saw none before: a spring of water. Their thirst can now be quenched; they can live. This incident in Hagar's life corresponds with a testimony African American Christians, particularly black women, have made for generations, that is, that God helped them make a way out of no way. Thus, one can conclude that God has often given African American people a new vision to see survival resources where they saw none before.

The third reason I think African Americans have appropriated the Hagar story is social. Hagar's family unit resembles a black family unit that has been current in the black community since slavery. That family unit is composed of a single female parent trying, without the father's presence and support, to raise her children. The Hagar story grounds the problem of this single-parent household precisely where it ought to be grounded: in the enslavement of African people. The enslavement of Africans in America inaugurated certain dis/membering cultural patterns cemented in place by public policies and laws that for generations worked against black people accumulating power. One of these dis/membering cultural patterns served to weaken the power of the black family structure by separating men from the family unit. During slavery this was done by selling black men (and women) away from their family units. Or the unit was weakened as white slave masters forced slave women to have sex with them, just as Hagar was forced to have sex with Abraham. Black male slaves had no power to stop the sexual exploitation of their sisters, wives, and mothers by white men. Mulatto children from this exploitation of black women were prevalent on many plantations, but the slavocracy enacted laws forbidding slave mothers who had been sexually exploited by these white men to tell the mulatto children who their true fathers were. In our own time, public assistance to poor black family units required that the father of the children not be a part of the family unit or the welfare would be stopped. There is no public policy of temporary assistance to families where the father is in the home and working but unable to obtain the kind of employment that would yield adequate financial resources for the sustenance of his family. Thus the "Hagars" in the African American community are quite visible as they struggle alone to make a way out of no way for themselves and their children without adequate financial resources.

African American traditions of biblical appropriation have been fundamental for what Professor Theophus H. Smith describes as black Americans "conjuring culture." In his book *Conjuring Culture: Biblical Formations of Black America*, Smith lifts up biblical themes and figures that have been important for black Americans as they transformed an alien and oppressive culture into a culture that was supportive of the black community's life and solidarity. Thus Smith describes the making of African American culture as " . . . a remarkable efficacious use of biblical figures, with historically transformative and therapeutic intent, in the social imagination and political performances of black North Americans."[1]

The African American Literacy Tradition

Since slavery, in both religious and secular areas of the African American community, the black literacy tradition has functioned to re/member the community's cultural heritage. Through poetry, prose, and drama, African American artists have produced works that function like mirrors in which the black community can see and critique itself.

The poet Paul Lawrence Dunbar, whose writing career extended from 1889 to 1906, used the black English of the folk so that the actual voice of the slave community would not be lost as processes of cultural assimilation got underway after slavery. The short-story writer Charles Chestnut, who also began his writing career in the nineteenth century, chose themes from black culture that kept aspects of the worldview of the slaves alive. He wrote stories showing the weak (a black person) outwitting a more powerful person (usually a white person). This corresponds with the theme from the African American folklore about Br'er Rabbit outwitting Br'er Fox—about the weak outwitting the more powerful.

Later writers such as Langston Hughes and Zora Neale Hurston produced literature that also kept alive language, themes, and characters that conveyed the worldview of a black cultural heritage. The humor that has been a vital survival tool for the black American community is captured by Langston Hughes in his creation of the character "Simple." The power, charisma, and manipulative politics of the black preacher are revealed in Zora Neale Hurston's creation of the character Rev. John in *Jonah's Gourd Vine*.[2] Richard Wright and James Baldwin, novelists of the mid- and late-twentieth century, grafted a protest voice on their portrayals of the oppression white America has meted out to black America. In some of their work these writers also provide critiques through characterization and plot design of the black community's way of dealing with this oppression. Margaret Walker, Alice Walker, Audre Lorde, and Toni Morrison integrate African American women's experience into American literary history, showing how black women have shaped culture, contributed to community solidarity, and kept family and church together.

The literary tradition—like the wisdom, education, and biblical appropriation traditions—has given black Americans a variety of clues for building and maintaining strong communities. Today, the struggle for the re/memberment of

---

1. Theophus H. Smith, *Conjuring Culture: Biblical Formations of Black America* (New York: Oxford University Press, 1994), p. 3.
2. Zora Neale Hurston, *Jonah's Gourd Vine* (New York: GK Hall & Co., 1998).

African American peoplehood is critical. The forces of dis/memberment have drained so much energy from the community. Drugs, dysfunctional public schools, ultraconservative forces in the courts and in Congress, the racist backlash now rampant in the United States, the growth and visibility of white hate groups targeting black people for attack—all these forces are hastening to dis/member African American peoplehood.

It is not easy to know what this new attack of dis/memberment means for black scholars today who are just beginning their teaching careers. I do know that the times, the crises, and the deaths of so many young people in the African American communities challenge us in ways that go beyond anything with which we are familiar. I suppose our hope is in the lessons we have learned from the giants like Professor Wilmore. Perhaps he would advise us to design creative strategies for re/memberment as we stand on the shoulders of our ancestors, mapping out liberation goals and plans in the faith that God stands with us and helps us to make a way out of no way. Perhaps we ourselves know that we will have to wrestle with both angels and devils before our African American community can be made whole. Perhaps we know that we must receive new vision before we can clearly distinguish angel from devil.

Questions for Thought and Discussion

1. What does the term "male oppression of females" mean to you as it relates to your religious experience?

2. How has sexism been practiced in the church? Or has it?

3. How are issues of genocide, education, and unemployment being addressed in your congregation? Or should they be addressed in your congregation? Why or why not?

4. Give an example of a situation where everyday life and humor have been used to tell stories.

5. Discuss education in your family. How was the church involved in the effort to educate?

6. What are some of the biblical themes and figures that are important to ethnic people?

7. Discuss your community's cultural heritage. Discuss your cultural heritage.

5 | The Ecumenical Legacy of Gayraud Wilmore
A Tribute to a Mentor

Thomas L. Hoyt, Jr.

IT IS MY distinct honor to contribute to this book in appreciation of one of our distinguished colleagues, a man of national and global renown, Gayraud Wilmore. He is my mentor in the ecumenical movement. For many years we have worked side by side in interchurch events at various places throughout the world. Gayraud Wilmore is and has been a trailblazer for the unity of the human family as the mission of the church. His ministry within the ecumenical movement has revolved around a double-edged question: "What is the price of unity without justice and justice without unity?"

Gayraud Wilmore's keen sense of unity and justice was kindled within the Civil Rights movement of the 1960s in the fight against racism. It was in the 1960s that he, like many of us, saw blacks and whites, Protestants, Catholics, Orthodox, and Jews marching together, singing together, eating together, going to jail together. The impression these things left on his future life and ministry was indelible.

What people were doing in the streets was facilitated by laws that were enacted in this country against racial segregation and discrimination. Action in the streets brought an awareness of injustice and helped to transform America. It was in the 1960s that the freedom movement reached its greatest strength. During that period we continued to earn freedom on the installment plan. In 1963, we achieved the right to public accommodations, we were given the right to vote by the Voting Rights Act of 1965, and we were granted the right to buy a house in any neighborhood by the Open Housing Act of 1968. We were still being victimized, however, by the tyranny of social designers who reduced public social consciousness to the level of a commodity spectacle, making it subject to cycles and vagaries of production, distribution, and consumption.

Interestingly enough, a form of political ecumenism was beginning to emerge in the religious arena, highlighted by the Decree on Ecumenism of Pope John XXIII on November 21, 1964. This opened up a dialogue that was intended to provide impetus for the Vatican's relationships and communion with confessions and fellow Christians who were not a part of the Roman Catholic Church.

Gayraud Wilmore was always there when the ecumenical world needed a leader and spokesperson who could speak with integrity and move the African American church community to action on the ecumenical front. He was there as a theological interpreter. In 1969 when James Forman stood in the sanctuary of the Riverside Church in New York City and demanded five hundred million dollars in reparations from white Christian churches and Jewish synagogues, it was the mild and gentle Gayraud Wilmore who wrote what some would call a radical statement about the theological meaning of the *Black Manifesto*, issued by Forman and the Black Economic Development Conference. Gayraud casti- gated the white church for failing to appreciate and demonstrate due respect for the theological value of black history and culture in the doing of Christian the- ology. He not only propagated this dissenting view in the Presbyterian Church, but also took it to an international forum.

He was there when Edler G. Hawkins and the black caucuses of the Presbyterian Church insisted on fair play within the predominantly white structures of that church and demanded the establishment of the first denomi- national Commission on Religion and Race in 1963. He has continually called for affirmative action or compensatory justice for those who have not had a fair opportunity within structures of both the church and the society. Concerning the domination of white European and American churches over the life and thought of nonwhite people, Gayraud had this to say:

> In the United States . . . African American Christians have struggled for more than two centuries to reinterpret and revise a distorted gospel that we received from white Christians who held us in bondage for almost two hundred fifty years and who then subjected us to one of the most degrading forms of racial segregation and discrimination that the world has ever known. The member churches of the World Council, the Roman Catholic Church, and other major denominations in Europe and North America might be obliged for some time to come to adopt compensatory policies and procedures to repair justly the injuries that blacks and other non-white ethnic groups suffered as a conse- quence of slavery, colonialism, neocolonialism, classism, and racism, officially and unofficially aided and abetted by Western Christianity.[1]

Gayraud recognized that equal justice was inherently unequal for those who for so long had been relegated to the margins of church life and secular society, so he advocated for compensatory justice. He was an active and criti- cal participant in the ecumenical movement, telling the world community to re- member its roots. He said: "The World Council of Churches, lest we forget, began with a solid commitment to racial justice as an indispensable requirement of the Christian unity it sought.[2]

---

1. Gayraud S. Wilmore and David T. Shannon, *Black Witness to the Apostolic Faith* (Grand Rapids: Wm. B. Eerdmans Publishing Co., 1985), p. vi.
2. Ibid.

The first Assembly of the World Council of Churches met in Amsterdam in 1948. The black American churches were present and helped shape the documents that came out of that and subsequent meetings. Yet, Professor Wilmore issued a stern warning to our white sisters and brothers in Christ: "The future of church unity may well depend upon the reappropriation of the spirit and intent of Amsterdam concerning deeds over words, visible fulfillment over specious promises, in the encounter between church and race."[3] He well understood that unity and justice were twins and that, in reality, there cannot be one without the other.

Even while working as a professor in predominantly white academic communities, Gayraud Wilmore was an active ecumenist. He did not suffer from what James H. Cone saw in some early proponents of black theology—an "accountability problem." Gayraud had asked and answered for himself "for what purpose and for whom" he did theology.[4] He was and remains responsible to the black church and the black community. It did not matter where he spoke or what he wrote; he represented the black church and community in the quest for justice and liberation.

In 1975 when the international ecumenical community needed someone who was respected, thoughtful, task-oriented, and fair, Gayraud Wilmore was invited to serve as moderator of the World Council of Churches (WCC) consultation in Europe on "Racism in Theology and Theology Against Racism." The document that developed from this consultation presented, in his words, "one of the most devastating criticisms of Christianity ever issued by an international conference of Christian theologians and social scientists."[5]

By his participation in this consultation Gayraud recognized that he had a chance to transform minds in the ecumenical movement. If one wanted a transformed mind, one had first to transform the vocabulary. The study on racism and theology developed by the Programme to Combat Racism and the Faith and Order movement of the World Council sought to eliminate negative and unfair words, judgments, and actions toward others. The participants in these units of the WCC and in the consultation on theology and racism knew that words affect behavior, that it was necessary to change how the ecumenical movement used words. This desire for a change in WCC vocabulary has been partially fulfilled in various church publications, textbooks, and in homiletical and liturgical language.

The consultation on "Racism in Theology and Theology Against Racism" sought to facilitate transformation through dialogue between competent

3. Ibid., p. vii.
4. See James H. Cone, *For My People* (Maryknoll, NY: Orbis Books, 1984), p. 26.
5. Wilmore and Shannon, eds., *Black Witness to the Apostolic Faith*, p. 10.

representatives of various churches. If one is to relate to any structure other than one's own, it is necessary to know what the other party is thinking. The consultation on racism opened up the issue of racial injustice in the context of faith and order. We need only recount the many international, national, and local dialogues between and among many churches across the world to show the relative influence of those who encountered and digested the document on racism.

The people who wrote the document wished to foster the social justice activities in race relations for the sake of the common good. In the 1960s many alliances for justice brought persons together across religious and denominational lines. Subsequent responses have usually been through various churches making their separate witnesses, whether through pastoral letters on nuclear warfare or on the inequities of the international economic situation. In light of a lack of initiative among some churches to foster cooperative work with respect to social justice in race relations, the drafters of the document on race and theology were wise to insist that real unity is impossible without real and transformative action on the part of churches willing to enter the public arena.

For the last forty-five years, Gayraud Wilmore has consistently worked for a unity that is predicated on justice-seeking ministries. In the United States he helped forge a fourth dimension for the word *ecumenical*. I describe the three discernible dimensions, or what we may call stages, of the evolution of the word *ecumenical* as follows. First, there was the geographic stage, with attendant cultural and political overtones. Second, there was the ecclesiastical stage which pointed toward a creedal orthodoxy. The third and most recent stage of development involved an attempt to define and fulfill "mission *and* unity" in the context of the worldwide Christian community. A fourth and contemporary stage or dimension of ecumenism involves recognition of the issues of human freedom, unity. Such an understanding of ecumenism recognizes that all humankind, the whole inhabited world or *oikoumene*, is needed for the full appropriation of God's self-disclosure as liberator in Jesus Christ.

It is in this fourth stage that Gayraud Wilmore and many others who live and work on the margins of the developed world have made a major contribution. In this fourth stage of ecumenical experience today, acknowledgment is made of the emerging reality of the so-called Third World and of the need and strategic importance of people who live "in the First World under Third World conditions." Every branch of the human family—women, blacks, Hispanics, other races and ethnic groups, the handicapped—all are now making their own distinctive contribution to our understanding of God and Christ. We are slowly coming to realize that the church includes people in all nations and cultures and that it cuts across every division of race, class, sex, and creed. At long last, Western Christians are beginning to affirm that the world includes many faiths, religions, and ideologies that we Christians dare not condemn, but with whom we must seek to share experiences and engage in dialogue and action, to the end that together we might discern through the Spirit what God is doing in the world.

Those who fail to recognize the significance of the broad diversity of persons and groups gathered up in the world ecumenical and who do not make room for the participation in the whole church remind me of the story about a group of blind men who visited the zoo. On their tour of the zoo they entered the elephant's cage to find out what manner of beast this was. One grabbed the tail, another the trunk, another one of the elephant's legs, and another an ear. The man who seized the tail declared the elephant to be like a rope; the man who felt the trunk thought him to be more like a horse; the man who touched the leg said the elephant was like a tree; and the man who handled the ear said he was more like a leaf. Having only one part of the picture, each drew the wrong conclusion.

Such has been the plight of the ecumenical movement. For many years it was blind to the experiences, perceptions, and traditions of those who viewed God and the world from the underside of history. Today, however, in place of the dominating *oikoumene* of a declining Roman Empire, we live in an emerging, interdependent world house of a global civilization that has diverse centers of power and influence. The real question on the ecumenical agenda today is this: Can human beings find a unity in the gospel that preserves their diversity, their distinctive qualities, but at the same time overcomes their separate idolatries?

Recognizing that unity with the oppressed and unity in extreme cultural diversity are foundational principles for the practice of true ecumenism today, Gayraud Wilmore issued a word of warning that the churches could well heed:

> [If we] assume that black culture and its religious component are irrelevant to the major Protestant and Roman Catholic traditions, the quest for Christian unity in the United States will be frustrated. As long as the massive presence of Afro-American ethnicity and the condition of the black population is ignored or neglected by the white churches of the United States, any discussion about Christian unity will lack cultural and theological realism—not to mention obedience to the will of God.[6]

Because the World Council of Churches recognized the deep commitment of Gayraud Wilmore and the respect that the American churches had for his integrity and leadership both here and abroad, he was asked in 1984, along with Dr. David Shannon, former president of Virginia Union University and Andover-Newton Theological Seminary, to co-chair a national conference of African American churches on the question of what it means to confess the Apostolic Faith today. There seems to have been a belief abroad in the World Council

---

6. Gayraud S. Wilmore, "Towards Visible Unity," Commission on Faith and Order, Lima, 1982, vol. II, Study Papers and Reports, World Council of Churches, Geneva, 1982, p. 149.

of Churches that if church leaders could only get their constituents to agree to confess together the Apostolic Faith as contained in the Nicene Creed, the churches would be that much closer to unity.

Unity as expressed by the confession of a common orthodoxy indicates what some people feel is the true meaning of ecumenical. As we have seen, however, in our times the word has been pushed beyond a mere statement of theological orthodoxy to a concern for justice expressed in collective action on behalf of those at the bottom of the social, economic, and political ladder.

Gayraud Wilmore, David Shannon, and scholars from twelve different American denominations gathered at Virginia Union University and developed the ecumenical document called "Toward a Common Expression of Faith: A Black North American Perspective." This statement was subsequently presented to the world community at the plenary meeting of the World Council of Churches Commission on Faith and Order in Stavanger, Norway, in August 1985. The document is now one of several circulating throughout the world dealing with a contemporary understanding of ecumenism. Those who make a practice of castigating African American ecumenists by asking "Why do you waste your time and energy in those endless discussions?" would do well to emulate people like Wilmore and Shannon. They saw the value of planting seeds, in the form of words and ideas, in the African American religious community and the World Council of Churches, so that they might germinate into deeds that move us all toward greater liberation and unity.

One of the questions raised by Gayraud Wilmore in his paper to the Richmond conference was this: How can we as African American churches and blacks within predominantly white denominations properly respond to the theme of church unity as an expression of the Apostolic Faith? We cannot do it apart from an analysis of the effect of racism on the way the faith is practiced by many white Christians and the manner in which blacks have responded to their racism. Inasmuch as racism is opposed to the Christian understanding of creation and redemption, the white church must seriously question whether it can be the church of the Christ and continue to engender a bias that denies the identity of a whole group of people.

African American churches refuse to permit apostolicity to be defined primarily as creedal conformity, as mere intellectual assent to the "verbal veracity" of the apostolic witness. The Richmond paper not only recognized the apostolicity of the faith that contemporary black Christians received from their illiterate slave ancestors, but it declared that "in the final analysis, the test of apostolicity is the experience of the life, death, and resurrection of Jesus Christ in our daily struggle against demonic powers that seek to rob us of our inheritance as children of God . . . our deeds, more than our creeds, determine whether we have fully received and acted upon the faith of the apostles." Confession of the Apostolic Faith comes out of a struggle with a believer's own personal and corporate experience, as he or she is informed by Scripture, tradition, and reason. It is out of this matrix that African Americans, in their own way, have confessed the Apostolic Faith as contained in the Nicene and Apostle's Creed, and inculcated in the world community of Christian believers for almost two thousand years.

Among black churches, the core test of apostolicity is not whether one recites these creeds or even is baptized, but whether one is able to carry out the apostolic task. Creed and deed must go together. There is an urgent call for theologians in the Faith and Order movement and member churches of the World Council of Churches to take more seriously the life, ministry, and teachings of Jesus Christ, which, when taken together, clearly identify him with those who are forgotten. Ecumenical theology has so concentrated on the Pauline corpus that the synoptic traditions of the New Testament have either dropped out of sight or have been relegated to a secondary role in ecumenical documents. We seem certain of the Christ of faith motif, but we are skeptical of the Jesus of history. It is as if we are afraid to let Jesus live among us because his presence in the midst of the poor and outcast might judge us too harshly.

Over forty representatives of the African American Christian churches and other churches around the world came together in Harlem, New York, in 1988. The consultation was prepared for and hosted by African American representatives of the historic black churches and African Americans representing predominantly white Protestant and Roman Catholic churches.[7] The purpose was to discuss the African American Christian contribution to the "Unity of the Church and the Renewal of the Human Community" study of the World Council of Churches Commission on Faith and Order. Gayraud Wilmore was one of the principal leaders of this historic event. Over the last thirty years, he has been on the cutting edge of ecumenical life, not only as a participant but as a strategist.

Thinking along these lines I am reminded of an experience that I and a group of my seminary classmates had in the 1960s. We left the Interdenominational Theological Center in Atlanta on our way to Selma, Alabama, in order to march with Dr. King. Tension was high and the times were dangerous. When we got to Montgomery someone suggested that we sing "We Shall Overcome." When we began to sing I saw police coming toward us swinging their clubs. I said to the young seminarians, "Let's get back on the bus, friends. We can sing "We Shall Overcome" on the bus."

My philosophy was that there is no sense in dying on the steps of the capitol building in Montgomery when one is trying to get to Selma. Sometimes it is

---

7. Throughout the document is an alternation between language referring to the same reality, "African American" and "Black" church. This language represents the different usages among the consultation participants to describe the church.

better to postpone an action in order to strike a more effective blow at a more opportune time.

Gayraud Wilmore is one who knows when to strike a blow for justice and when to hold back until that more opportune time comes. He recently said to me, "You cannot fight every battle, and anyway, it's not a good idea to fight too much." He is a strategic fighter who chooses his own dying ground. This takes patience. With respect to the quest for Christian unity, it takes a patience and wisdom grounded in the truth of the Word of God that unity is a gift rather than mere human effort. The unity of the church, because it is a mystery and an act of God, will not result from plans of men and women, even though we certainly must plan. The unity of the household of faith will come in moments of surprise, in unexpected places and ways. We indeed must plan for Christian unity, but we plan knowing that the results are ultimately in the hands of God.

In ecumenical contexts, deep commitments call for the gift of sharing pain. I have seen Gayraud in pain when he tells the story of his disappointment in the World Council Commission on Faith and Order consultations in the United States by African Americans. That pain is almost palpable when he writes: "The *WCC Statements and Actions on Racism, 1948–79*, edited by Ans. J. van der Bent (Geneva, 1980), did not include the first chapter of the original report of "Racism in Theology and Theology Against Racism" that came out of the 1975 consultation. Was that section of the report eliminated from the official collection of WCC policy statements on race because it was one of the most critical analyses of racism in the European and North American churches ever promulgated in an ecumenical document on theology?"[8]

In the most ordinary circumstances it takes "a-summering and a-wintering" of two parties for each to trust the other with their stories of pain. But in bilateral and multilateral, and in global and ecumenical contexts, trust comes slowly through a movement from parochialism to ecumenism. In the midst of sharing painful stories of disunity, our vocation is to know when to listen, when to touch, when to respond, and when to care.

I will never forget the pain I experienced at a meeting of the World Council of Churches when a member of a sister church announced to us that it would be impossible for them to offer us the communion cup, but if we believed them wrong that we should pray for them. They then proceeded to give Communion to each other. When the main enactment of the Eucharist was over, the rest of us were offered bread that had been blessed and was being shared as a sign of brokenness and pain in the present and a sign of hope for the future. The pain, which can be a gift of God when shared, will be all too common in the days ahead. But we must struggle on in hope.

---

8. Wilmore and Shannon, eds., *Black Witness to the Apostolic Faith*, p. 10.

Continual commitment to the ecumenical task calls for the gift of sharing not only pain, but also creative encounters with God through worship built on the traditions, liturgies, music, and faith languages of many believing communities. Such an experience of worship has about it a "whole earth" quality, one that transcends the one-note parochialism of our life. We must learn anew that spirituality must be at the heart of the ecumenical movement. It is significant, for example, that the spirituals and the gospel songs of the black tradition are understood and appreciated in various cultures around the world. When Gayraud and I attended a meeting of the World Council of Churches in Stavanger, Norway, we were keenly aware that music transcends national boundaries. White youth in that setting knew and could sing the gospel music of Andrae Crouch better than we could!

Commitment to the ecumenical movement brings with it the gift of friendship. This follows the pattern of Jesus, who told his disciples, "I do not call you servants any longer, because the servant does not know what his mother is doing; but I have called you friends, because I have made known to you everything that I have heard from my Father" (John 15:15).

The call is for us to recognize the value and rewards of friendship—love being the overriding character of the relationship. Friendships take time—walking time, time at the table, idle time, time to savor common experience, and worship time. As we live and work with ecumenical friends, experiences of "my house" and "your house" move toward "our home." Protestants and Roman Catholics have had mind-changing experiences because of friendships developed in ecumenical dialogue. Through these experiences, and the commitments that come out of them, we will be transformed to become a new creation, sharing our gifts of the Spirit for the life of the world.

Those of us whom God has permitted to work in the worldwide ecumenical movement dream of a church that will not become one with the world because of its power, but will have an ever stronger influence in the world because of its integrity, a church that will command the respect of the powerful and give them a vision of a new world of peace and justice. We dream of a church that will be a community where God is truly known, where faith is not merely an intellectual exercise, but the fruit of the experience of grace. We dream of a church in which the ecumenical fellowship of scholarship will continue to provide the intellectual basis for documents like the justly famous World Council consensus on "Baptism, Eucharist, and Ministry" and other statements and ecumenical actions that make for the unity and transformation of both individuals and societies.

Finally, we dream of a church that will be truly inclusive, where the faithfulness of ministry will be shared by women and men, rich and poor, liberal and conservative, educated and handicapped, and those who do not consider themselves to be so. All one in Christ Jesus. And a community not only inclusive, but also caring, a community whose highest priority is working and living under the gospel to meet human needs.

I, along with other ecumenists, bemoan the fact that our mentor, Gayraud Wilmore, has greatly curtailed his activity in the ecumenical movement. Nevertheless, we will not forget a statement both prophetic and challenging that he addressed to the ecumenical movement:

> Afro-American Christians, both those within black denominations and those within predominantly White denominations, have not been conspicuous in the World Council of Churches studies of Faith and Order. From all indications we will be even less represented in the future because the increasing membership of the Council and the necessity of giving greater voice to Third World churches and women will probably reduce the proportional representation and visibility of black Americans in the years to come . . . but we must accept some responsibility for our marginality in the World Council of Churches. This means that if an Afro-American Christian experience and perspective is to have any impact on the world ecumenical movement it will require our theologians to take a more active role in responding to the WCC studies and initiatives. Indeed, we must take the initiative ourselves and place before the Council and the world confessional bodies the problems and issues we deem important to the mission and unity of the church at this point in time.[9]

The Reverend Stephen J. Sidorak, Jr., Executive Director of the Christian Conference of Connecticut, concluded his annual report to the Connecticut Conference by retelling an event that occurred at the Seventh Assembly of the World Council of Churches in Canberra, Australia. I too experienced the particular event of which he spoke and will close with his words:

> Joan Campbell of the National Council of Churches of Christ in the U.S.A., had an exchange with Philip Potter, former General Secretary of the WCC. Joan asked Philip if he would "define the characteristics that a leader must possess in order to help others deal with the serious times in which we find ourselves."
>
> Philip responded: "If you are going to be a leader in this time, there are three things that you must have: You must have a screw loose, you must have a death wish, and you must have a sense of humor."

That was not exactly what the crowd expected, and you could hear them collectively draw a startled breath—then with that half smile that is so characteristic of him, Philip said, "Perhaps I should exegete the text. To have a screw loose is to be open to the movement of the Spirit in your life—not to have life so carefully planned that the Spirit can't gain access. To have a death wish is to be clear that the choice to be a shepherd is to reject the crown for a cross. And

---

9. Ibid., p. 16.

to have a sense of humor is an absolute necessity to ward off the Devil, for the Devil never laughs."

With indebtedness to Steve Sidorak for reminding me of that exchange between Philip Potter and Joan Campbell, I conclude with three hopes that I have for Gayraud Wilmore. I hope he will remain open to the promptings of the Holy Spirit in our midst. I hope he will always remember that it is not organization's efforts, but God that we seek to glorify, and if our witness is faithful, we are likely to suffer for it. And finally, I hope he will do everything in his power to keep forcing that frown on the Devil's face!

Questions for Thought and Discussion

1. What is your stand on the issue of affirmative action? Discuss whether you feel it has helped or hindered church and society.

2. Describe a situation where negative, unfair words, judgments, and actions toward others have affected the life of those in the church.

3. How has your church fostered social-justice activities in race relations?

4. How has your church been involved in ecumenical events?

5. Does your congregation recite the creeds of your denomination?

6. Have you experienced being denied the elements at a communion service? Describe the experience.

7. Have you experienced being excluded in any way as part of the worship experience?

6 | Theological Ideas Gone Awry
The Shaping of American Racism*
Paul R. Griffin

I AM PLEASED to have been invited to contribute to this book honoring Professor Gayraud S. Wilmore. I personally experienced his demanding scholarship when he edited the revised edition of my book *The Struggle for a Black Theology of Education: Pioneering Efforts of Post Civil War Clergy* (Atlanta: ITC Press, 1993). It is in recognition of his life and work that I humbly dedicate this chapter on the role of theological ideas in the shaping of American racism.

Like many across this land, I have been exceedingly troubled by the resurgence of racial bigotry that has occurred over the past two decades. Like others, I had believed that the decades of the 1960s and 1970s would bring the monster to its deathbed. We were wrong! American racism has fully recovered and is alive and doing quite well today. Writing this chapter on the revival of the demon, as sobering a prospect as that thought is for all of us who worked so hard for its demise, nevertheless, has been excellent therapy for both body and soul.

I want to make clear, first of all, that although I use the term *religionist* to refer to Christian, what I have to say about their role in creating and nourishing American racism also applies to many non-Christian religionists.

Second, I want to define American racism as a persistent and widely held creed or doctrine that some people are innately inferior to other people, and that God, nature, or some inexorable force of history made those unfortunate people that way. American racism as an ideological construct also expresses itself by unjust concrete actions in society, actions backed by dominating political and economic power. Third, I want to propose this thesis: that American racism is today—and has always been—a religion. It is a religion because it has been anchored in racist theological thought and distorted biblical ideas that over the past four hundred years became uncontestable divine truths in American culture.

I

Until recently, we have given little attention to religion's role in shaping and sustaining racism. There are a variety of reasons for this inattention, but the

---

*This chapter is adapted by permission of Pilgrim Press. Copyright © 1999 from *Seeds of Racism in the Soul of America*, by Paul R. Griffin.

energy it has taken simply to survive the storms of racial violence has been one major distraction for black people. Because of the long history and intensity of the struggle against acts of racial bigotry in this land, African Americans have often lost sight of the fact that American racism is as much a matter of ideas or ideologies as of actual racist deeds. Our blindness in this regard has frequently caused us to misinterpret the essence of racism as being first and foremost an economic, social, or political problem. Interpreting racism in this manner has deceived us about its true nature. We have persuaded ourselves that this evil can be overcome by confronting it as if it were merely concrete acts rather than ideas. Even Dr. Martin Luther King Jr., as insightful a race leader as he was, occasionally suffered from this blindness. But at his best, Dr. King realized that his long and arduous struggles against concrete racist practices and systems were having little success erasing bigotry from this society. He wrote, for example:

> [In] the final analysis, the problem of race in America is not a [social, economic, or] political one. It is a moral issue . . . and the white church must face its historic obligations in this racial crisis. . . . The task of conquering racism, therefore, is an inescapable *must* confronting the white church today. . . . The church must get to the ideational roots of racial hatred, something that the law cannot accomplish.[1]

It is clear that in his later years King realized the taproot of American racism was buried not in racist practices that can easily be perceived by eye and ear. The situation is much more complex than that. The root of this pernicious disease is found in historic racist theological and biblical interpretations.

The year 1968, when Dr. King was assassinated in Memphis, Tennessee, was also the year of the publication of a book that provided great insight into the historic interconnectedness between American religion and racism. The book was *The Unheavenly City Revisited* by Professor Edward C. Banfield, whose teaching career included tenure at three of the most prestigious universities in this country—Harvard University, the University of Chicago, and the University of Pennsylvania. It is no mere coincidence that in the same year Banfield's book was published, President Richard Nixon appointed him to chair a task force on the federal Model Cities program that had been initiated under the administration of President Lyndon Baines Johnson. As is commonly known, Johnson began Model Cities as a part of his vision of a "Great Society" from which the disease of racism would be extirpated. The charge to Banfield's task force was to evaluate Model Cities and recommend whether or not it was worthy of being continued under Nixon. Banfield prevailed on the task force to recommend overwhelmingly that the program be discontinued with the utmost dispatch. This recommendation was not simply a pragmatic economic, social, or political

---

1. Martin Luther King Jr., *Stride Toward Freedom* (New York: Ballantine Books, 1958), p. 167. Italics mine.

policy judgment. It reeked of racist theological ideas that had been the corner-stone of American polity for nearly four hundred years.

Although not an ordained clergy person, the very title that Banfield chose from his massive publication confirms that race influenced and controlled his historic religious theories. The frontispiece of his book contains a quotation from one of the nation's most heralded late seventeenth- and early eighteenth-century white clergymen, none other than the celebrated Puritan divine, the Reverend Cotton Mather:

> Come hither, and I will show you, an admirable Spectacle! 'Tis an Heavenly City. . . . A City to be inhabited by an Innumerable Company of Angels, and by the spirits of Just Men . . . *Put on thy beautiful Garments,* O America, the Holy City [of God]![2]

As a scholar of urban studies and political science, Professor Banfield was well aware of a historical fact that has often been forgotten or intentionally omitted in discussions of the role of religion in American life. From the moment Europeans first confiscated this country to this very day, the theological ideas of the American religionist have not only shaped but have also deeply infused everything in this country—economics, politics, education, mass culture, and the most everyday human routines. It does not require a quantum leap of schol-arly speculation to assert that religious ideas have also historically defined and guided American racism. Although separated by almost four centuries from the Reverend Mather and other early white religionists who shared his ideas, Banfield was determined to recover both the spirit and the letter of their early vi-sion of America. He was dogged about restoring this dream because he was fear-ful that something terrifying was happening to it. I believe that in his view, this horrifying thing was that Model Cities and other affirmative-action programs and federal antidiscrimination enactments were giving black city dwellers some real hope of finally becoming a part of this nation.

What was the content of that generative vision of Banfield's ancestors? Con-trary to what history books have seduced many into believing—particularly the writings of Northern white scholars—neither racism nor slavery during the colonial period began in the South. Both had their origins in the North, among highly enlightened and cultured white Christians commonly called the Puritans or, as they thought of themselves, the "people of God." These pious Christians did not—as Winthrop Jordan suggests—"rather mindlessly" fall into initiating racism and slavery as black people's lot in this country.[3] Their intro-duction of these twin evils was the result of much careful and serious delibera-

2. Edward C. Banfield, *The Unheavenly City Revisited* (Boston: Little, Brown and Com-pany: 1974), p. iii.
3. Winthrop D. Jordan, *White Over Black: American Attitudes Toward the Negro, 1550–1812* (Baltimore: Penguin Books, 1969), p. 67.

tion. The Puritans' creation of these dual monsters was, in part, the result of who they understood themselves to be. They were a fervently religious people who seized this land because of two equally passionate and steadfast convictions. The first was that God had made them God's new "chosen people." The second was that God had given them a "special covenant to make America God's City Set on a hill and a Beacon to the Rest of the World."

Even on their maiden voyage to New England, puritan leaders such as John Winthrop, the first governor of the Massachusetts Bay Colony, were boldly announcing:

> The work we have in hand . . . is by mutual consent, through a special overruling providence and a more than an ordinary approbation of the churches of Christ. . . . [This work is to build] a place of cohabitation and consortship. . . . Thus, stands the cause between God and us: we are entered into a covenant with Him for this work.[4]

Given this powerful theological confession, we would like to believe that the Puritans were coming here to create an inclusive or a multiracial society, a nation where people of all colors would live and work together to build God's kingdom on earth. Americans, generally, have been loath to believe that these devout Christians were committed to the establishment of a system of racism and slavery that would deliberately exclude people of color from equal participation in their lofty enterprise. Here we learn two important lessons about the nature of American racism. The first is that much of what is said "ain't" what is meant, and much of what appears to be "ain't what it be." The second lesson is that when a racist finds no easily accessible way for acting out his or her racism, he or she will always shrewdly make a way out of no way. This certainly was the case with the early Puritans. Their words sound as if they were committed to the creation of an America where all of God's children—white and black, red and yellow, tan and cream-colored—would live and work together as equals. Their actions, however, quickly exposed the racist ideology that was really forming in their minds.

In those pious Christian minds were ideas that smacked of nothing but an unfounded and extreme hatred of black people. These patterns of thought had been implanted in their minds long before the Puritans first set foot on these shores. They had been sown and cultivated by European voyagers who had traveled to Africa during the late fifteenth and early sixteenth centuries. Landing in what they called the "Dark Continent," these travelers encountered a people they had never seen before. But instead of trying to get to know them, they immediately denigrated their humanity by identifying them as a

---

4. John Winthrop, *A Model of Christian Charity*, in *The American Puritans: Their Prose and Poetry*, edited by Perry Miller (New York: Anchor Books, 1956), p. 82.

"black, mysterious, heathenish, oversexed, evil, lazy, and smelly people who are strangely different to our superior white race."[5]

Among these voyagers was a fellow countryman of the Puritans, Richard Hakluyt, who, when he returned to England, wrote of his travels and instilled in his colleagues' minds the racist ideas he had maliciously formulated about Africans.

A brief excursus here may be helpful. When we first hear new ideas we don't always know when or how they might become useful in the future. Moreover, because relatives, friends, teachers, or other authority figures are usually the source of these newly discovered ideas, we sometimes accept them blindly as if they were some kind of gospel truths. The consequence is that regardless of whether such new ideas are true or false, if they are frequently heard they will more than likely take up permanent residence in our unconscious minds until the right moment comes along. It is in such situations or moments that we activate these dormant thoughts and use them to rationalize or justify our actions.

When the Puritans settled here, they did so determined to build a holy commonwealth that would be a lighthouse for the rest of the world. But it is one of the critical developments in the history of American racism that when these pious Christians spoke of building a holy empire, their words did not mean they had any plans to include black people as equal members of their self-proclaimed heavenly city. They had no such intentions because they came to this new land with their subconscious minds already filled with racist preconceptions about black men and women.

II

As the professedly chosen race, the problem for the Puritans should have been how it was possible that they could fulfill their self-proclaimed covenant to construct a heavenly city, and at the same time either enslave or exclude blacks. This problem should have been particularly vexing for the Puritans because they were a highly learned people who were well aware that reason, philosophy, science, law, history, and theology all affirmed that God created all human beings and entitled them to the same freedoms and human rights. They should have known that acts of oppression against, and the subjugation of, Africans or any other group in their holy empire would defy rationality and the Natural Law. Such acts would also blaspheme the name of their God and stain the Christian tradition. But recalling that racists are skilled in making a way even when there appears to be none, the Puritans devised a crafty theological way of justifying their enslavement and ostracism of Africans. This they accomplished by

5. See Richard Hakluyt, *The Principal Navigations, Voyages, Traffiques and Discoveries of the English Nation* (London: J. M. Dent and Sons, Ltd., reprint 1903).

tying the racist ideas that had long resided in their minds to their ethnocentric interpretations of the Bible and Christian theology.

Three biblical and theological doctrines were invoked by the Puritans to define and defend their racist behavior. First, they turned to the doctrine of Creation, giving it a racist twist so that, as the argument ran, when God created humankind, God not only created multiple races, but created them hierarchically.

> God Almighty, in his most holy and wise providence hath so disposed of the Condition of mankind, that in all times some must be rich some poor, some high and eminent in power and dignity; others mean and in subjection.[6]

Naturally they insisted that white people were at the top of the hierarch because God had made them the most pious, intelligent, powerful, and cultured of all people. A second theological notion that they found useful for their purposes was in the doctrines of election and covenant. Again turning to the King James Version of the Bible, they drew on the law codes in Lev. 25:45–46, which read as follows:

> Both thy bondmen, and thy bondmaids, which thou shalt have, shall be of the heathen that are round about you; . . . Moreover, of the children of the strangers that do sojourn among you, of them shall ye buy, and of their families that are with you, which they begat in your land: and they shall be your possession. . . . They shall be your bondmen for ever.[7]

The Puritans cited these verses to prove that because God had commanded the ancient Hebrews to capture and enslave any uncovenanted and heathen stranger who dwelt in their Promised Land, they, the Puritans, were under the same decree since they were God's new chosen people.

The third theological idea the Puritans used was the doctrine of sin and double predestination. Again they found in Genesis—chapters 9 and 10—a story they could twist for their own purposes so that the curse of Canaan became a convenient justification for the proposition that God had predestined the black race to be the most abject sinners of all human races.

These racist interpretations of the doctrines of Creation, covenant, sin, and predestination are among the major theological ideas that have helped to shape and sustain American racism over the centuries. The American Puritans put their own spins on these doctrines, which enabled them to advance two theological rationalizations for why black people should not be a part of their holy commonwealth. On one hand, the doctrines of Creation and covenant enabled them to assert a divine right to enslave the "heathenish" blacks. They could claim this right because of a holy privilege that was collateral with God having

6. Miller, ed., *The American Puritans*.

7. Lev. 25:45–46, KJV.

created them the "most high, eminent and dignified" race in the divine hierarchy of humankind. God had providentially invested them with absolute dominion over blacks, who were the lowest and most heathenish race in "God's great Chain of Being." One of the earliest examples of this claim is found in the thoughts of Theophilus Eaton, the first governor of the Connecticut Colony. In 1643 Eaton boasted that he had been holding blacks in bondage for some time because God's commands in Leviticus made it his divine right and duty to capture and enslave these "strange and savage Africans until death do us part."

On the other hand, their manipulation of the doctrine of sin and predestination gave the Puritans a theological framework for propagating one of the most vicious denials of black humanity that racists have ever concocted. They argued that their treatment of black people was consistent with God's will. But going even further, they claimed that the enslavement and segregation of black people by Christians was in reality of invaluable benefit—a literal godsend—to these allegedly inferior men and women.

History has long since taught us that on those occasions when some whites insist they are being of invaluable benefit to blacks, it is past time to slip on our Air Jordans and start running as fast as we can in the other direction. Anyone who has not yet learned this lesson should delve again into the writings of the Reverend Cotton Mather. Justifying his own slaveholding as well as that of his New England Puritan compatriots, Mather preached that God had never ordained blacks to be anything other than slaves to white Christians. It is time, he announced, that these "miserable [black] children of Adam and Noah" understand that if they will only—

> serve God patiently and cheerfully in the Condition of slavery which he orders for them, then their condition will very quickly be infinitely mended in eternal happiness when they get to heaven.[8]

This quote established beyond a shadow of a doubt that the Puritans must stand accused of having planted some of the most bigoted theological ideas that have terrorized black people for the past four hundred years. Second, it brings us full circle back to Professor Edward C. Banfield and why that distinguished modern scholar chose this much-heralded Puritan clergyman as his intellectual paragon.

Professor Banfield titled his book *The Unheavenly City Revisited*, because he was convinced that his ancestors' vision of a lily-white "heavenly city," thanks to Lyndon Johnson's Model Cities program, was becoming a real-life nightmare. The decades of the 1960s seemed to Banfield to be foreboding that for the first time in its history America was finally moving away from the historic theo-

---

8. Cotton Mather, *The Negro Christianized: An Essay to Excite and Assist that Good Work, The Instruction of Negro Servants in Christianity* (Boston: B. Green, 1706), p. 69.

logical ideas that black people were indisputably inferior to whites and thus were obliged, by God's immutable decree, to accept the status of outsiders or "strangers in this holy land."

III

White religion, at least in the early 1960s, played a considerable role in pushing the nation toward an apparently new and, for Banfield and others, an unwelcome direction. National governing bodies of the major denominations— particularly the Episcopalians, the United Methodists, the United Church of Christ, the Presbyterians, and the Lutherans—seemed to be encouraging their local churches to rise up and take a firm stand against theologically informed racism. These churches, which had picked up the torch of Puritan theological racism around the mid-1700s, now indicated that they were finally ready to disavow the ideas that their Puritan predecessors had made a pillar of American culture. Mainstream white religionists walked at the head of the black protest marches, convened seminars on racism, and even contributed large sums of money to the Southern Christian Leadership Conference and other black Civil Rights groups.

For the first time in American history, rampant and brutal hatred of black people seemed to be waning. Acts of violence that had routinely either enslaved, segregated, or otherwise terrorized millions of blacks for nearly four centuries, seemed to be coming to an end. The segregation and discrimination that began with the Puritans and violently swept across this heavenly city until the 1960s, appeared to be crumbling like the walls of Jericho. Economic, social, and political doors that had been slammed shut now began to open—albeit with persistent and loud creaking. Academic institutions that had long aided efforts to deny African American youth the opportunities of higher education and keep them social and intellectual second-class citizens, began vigorously to recruit them. They even sought black professors and top administrators, although frequently they used the proverbial excuse that qualified African Americans were extremely rare and difficult to retain. Some whites who had spat in our faces now joined us in the struggle to expose and abolish American racism.

The apparent willingness of some white church people to finally cast aside the old ideas that had long upheld the vision of America as a lily-white heavenly city was more than hard-core racists could bear. Almost everywhere Banfield and his like-minded colleagues turned, they saw old racial ideas coming under what appeared to be a lethal attack. They were terrified at the possibility that the historic roots of American racism were doomed to extinction in the late twentieth century. They then saw as their urgent task, during the decades of the 1970s and 1980s, to turn back the tide. Hence, they sought to incite the white masses into reviving and restoring their ancestors' vision of making this nation a City of God where the affirmation of black humanity could be viewed not only as a social error, but also as a theological sin. Banfield's books show that he was convinced that the most rapid and easiest way to accomplish this would be to resuscitate the Puritan ideal. After all, he reasoned, racist ideas are as American as apple pie—indelible ideological props of the American ethos.

A parenthetical comment about ideas seems appropriate here. Ideas—particularly after they have become widespread theological beliefs—carry, as Plato taught, a certain "eternality" that makes their total eradication virtually impossible. Racist ideas are buttressed by a masterfully cunning ability to change their faces when their alleged sacredness is threatened by powerful transformations in a society. It is this ability to shrewdly transfigure itself that has given theologically informed racism a special kind of immortality in American culture.

Although he was not a clergyman, Professor Banfield was well aware that he could not hope to turn white liberals and the masses they were beginning to influence against African Americans by simply restating the ethnocentric theories of the distant past. Under the impact of King's movement, the revolutionary changes that had occurred in the attitudes and policies of the mainstream Christian churches had seriously undermined the sacredness of those old ideas. In order to revive the Puritans' ideas of race, Banfield gave those ideas a new face by skillfully disguising his book as an urban studies analysis, a pragmatic evaluation of the effectiveness of Model Cities. Accordingly, he proposed that the program was proving to be not only ineffective, but also a threat to the hallowed vision of what America should be, precisely because it encouraged the continuation of the blight and urban decay that, in his view, was defiling this nation as God's New Jerusalem.

Following in the footsteps of his Puritan ancestors, Professor Banfield brazenly rejected the notion that white racism plays any role in the persistence of the urban pestilence and disintegration that he claimed were destroying the land of his forebears. In his view, African Americans are the fundamental cause of this scourge and corruption. Here is a classic example of the ability of theologically informed racism to perpetuate itself by changing its face when its existence is threatened. Banfield knew that blaming African Americans outright for urban decay would find little support in light of the dramatic changes in white America's perception of social problems during the 1960s. Thus, instead of directly invoking the Puritan theory that black people's sins caused them to be outsiders in God's holy land, he recast that old idea under the rubric of what he calls the "imperatives of class culture." By "class culture" he means a state or condition governed by our innate psychological abilities rather than by external social forces. He categorizes human beings on the basis of their inborn psychological capacities to "plan for the future." Thus, upper-class human beings are those born with a native ability to plan for the future, while lower-class human beings are born psychologically unable to plan or even think beyond the present. In his own words:

> The lower-class individual lives from moment to moment. . . . Impulse governs his behavior, either because he cannot discipline himself to sacrifice a present for a future satisfaction, or because he has no sense of the future. He is therefore radically improvident. . . . His bodily needs (especially for sex) and his taste for action, take precedence over everything else—and certainly any work routine. He works only as he must to stay alive, and drifts from one unskilled job to another, taking no [enduring] interest in the work.[9]

IV

In 1701, the Puritan John Saffin—a Boston jurist, businessman, and slaveholder—published the first massive defense of racism and slavery in America, *A Brief and Candid Answer to a Late Printed Sheet, Entitled, The Selling of Joseph*. Saffin poetically portrays blacks in this fashion:

> Cowardly and cruel are those Blacks Innate,
> Prone to Revenge, Imp of inveterate hate.
> He that exasperates them, soon espies
> Mischief and murder in their very eyes.
> Libidinous, Deceitful, False and Rude,
> The Spume Issue of Ingratitude.
> The Premises consider'd, all may tell
> How near good Joseph they are parallel.[10]

There is a historic relationship between Saffin's and Banfield's racist depictions of black people. They shared the dream of a heavenly city that would be eternally a multilayered, multicultured land where persons of African descent would be forever subordinated as innately immoral and ungodly strangers.

In view of the positive changes in the racial attitudes of many white religionists during the 1960s and 1970s, one would have expected that white liberals, men and women, would have risen up in indignation against Banfield and other racist intellectuals. Unfortunately, this was not the case. Banfield's refacing of the old Puritan theological confessions of racism attracted widespread support among religionists such as Jerry Falwell, Bob Jones, Jr., Pat Robertson, and others. In varying ways these men of the cloth rose up to defend Banfield's views. Like him they were convinced that white America was rapidly becoming an *unheavenly* city because of the alleged psychological bent of black people for moral depravity. Thus, each of these professed guardians of American's sacred

---

9. Banfield, *The Unheavenly City Revisited*, p. 61.

10. George H. Moore, *Notes on the History of Slavery in Massachusetts* (New York: D. Appleton Company, 1866), p. 252.

mission burst with Banfield to give cunning new faces to the historic Puritan theological ideas of race. For example, during this period, the Reverend Bob Jones, Jr., built his Bob Jones University in Greenville, South Carolina, assuring white parents that it would be a refuge for their daughters, securing them from African American males who could not control their irresponsible sexual appetites. The Reverend Jerry Falwell built the Moral Majority movement on the blustery proposition that white America needed to redirect itself backwards, lest it become what he delighted in calling a modern-day Sodom and Gomorrah—familiar code words for cities dominated by uncontrollable black masses. The Reverend Pat Robertson inundated the airwaves and print media with affirmations of the Puritan notion that America can never become that "heavenly city" as long as African Americans are indulged in with federal entitlement programs such as Model Cities.

Many fair-minded persons will insist that Falwell, Jones, and company are the worst examples of white religious zealots and do not accurately represent the liberal white religionist who joined the Civil Rights movement of the 1960s. But let us probe more deeply and see whether the so-called progressive religionists are guilty of many of the same disingenuous charges that are being leveled against blacks today by their right-wing fellow believers.

At first glance it is not easy to discern the guilt of the liberal religious community because many liberals have learned how to be a tad bit more deceptive with their racism. On closer scrutiny, however, one finds that many progressives are not less culpable than hard-core racists when it comes to blaming the victims of American racism. Many white religionists who would disavow the company of the persons named above are what I would call compensatory white liberals. That is to say, they are persons who frequently pursue ways to compensate for concrete racist practices by cosmetic and superficial adjustments in the status quo, but who strongly refuse to support any remedies that propose to radically address and correct the racist activities of the past four centuries.

As Dr. King sat in a jail cell in Birmingham, Alabama, charged with civil disobedience, eight white clergymen sent him a letter. Although he does not tell us whether or not these Catholic, Protestant, and Jewish clerics actually participated in the demonstrations for which he was incarcerated, he does say they were not overt haters of black people, not the inveterate bigots one finds in the Ku Klux Klan or other dyed-in-the-wool racist organizations. Once he had received the letter of those pious and otherwise progressive religionists, he saw them for what they really were—liberal compensators. They did not write to propose a prayer meeting with him or to inquire how he was holding up in the squalor and misery of a jail cell. They certainly did not write to affirm his open denunciation of American racism. They wrote, first of all, to label him as an "extremist and outsider" who had wrongly invaded their heavenly city of Birmingham and had incited chaos and ungodliness with his radical plea for black equality. Second, they wrote King to denounce his protests as being both "unwise and untimely."

It was only after Dr. King defied Birmingham's laws and identified the city's segregation as a historic moral issue rooted in racist theological ideas, that these liberal religionists turned their voices against him. Until he began to talk about racism as being steeped in religious ideas, they gave every indication that they were genuinely sympathetic to the African American quest for social justice. King even praised them as "intelligent men who showed goodwill toward Negroes." While these liberal religionists initially were willing at least to empathize with King's struggle and were willing to compensate for the sins of the past by showing "goodwill towards Negroes," they could not bring themselves to denounce American racism for what it really is—a theologically informed ideological construct that continues to play itself out in concrete acts of violence against black people.

We should not take the fact lightly that the minds of some liberal religionists have become so impregnated with these constructs that they are no longer aware of their bias. We regard this failure to recognize racism for what it is with utmost seriousness because some religious and secular liberals are pressing hard for "multicultural strategies" that have recently come into vogue but skillfully bypass the fundamental question of anti-black racism. Multiculturalism can be defined as a movement grounded in three basic strategies: (1) accepting people of diverse cultures; (2) affirming every group's (or in some cases, individual's) God-given or natural right to be what they want to be; and (3) demonstrating reverence for the common humanity of all people, regardless of their race, ethnicity, gender, or sexual preference.

While on the surface multiculturalism would appear to hold some promise for helping us bring an end to the long chapter of American racism, it is proving itself basically incapable of that accomplishment. So many white liberals have a double standard when it comes to applying multiculturalism's three strategies in a way that comes to terms with the ideational confessions of the past. This double standard is obvious when, on the one hand, liberals will eagerly and boldly argue the merits of every other racial, ethnic, and gender group's pleas for full inclusion in the society, while on the other hand, resist either listening to or acting on the agonized and sustained cries of the black masses for relief from the racist policies and practices that continue to keep them at the bottom of the well.

In recent years, liberal religionists have come forward to heed the pleas of some Americans that certain sacred confessions deny their humanity and condemn them to the status of outsiders. For example, they have applauded the efforts of white feminist theologians to cast aside the male label for God and adopt biblical and theological language that makes God either a gender-multiple deity (mother and father) or one who is completely gender-neutral. These same liberal religionists, however, have stubbornly ignored the petitions of black men and women for relief from the sacred codes and creeds of American racism that have for so long tormented them and wreaked havoc with their self-esteem.

Because of the failure to take seriously black pleas for social, political, and economic justice, we must find many liberal religionists no less guilty than conservatives for the perpetuation of historic racist ideas. Their evident refusal to rise up against scholars and clerics who would renovate those ideas to help restore the racist vision of the past, renders them equally reprehensible with those who openly propagate that vision.

Notwithstanding all the verbiage about multiculturalism during the past few years, many white liberals simply have not been able or willing to cleanse their minds of the racist ideas planted by their ancestors. Until they do, there is little hope that the race problem in America will ever be solved. As Martin King warned us almost thirty years ago, the task of conquering racism is an inescapable *must* confronting the white church. White religion must shoulder this awesome responsibility because it was the first to provide the theological foundation for this peculiar brand of religious racism. By making racism a religion, the churches made it also a moral issue. Morality, as we all know, cannot be legislated. It requires a conversion: It is clear today that white Christianity, and much of Judaism, for that matter, have not yet converted themselves from adhesion to the ideational substructure of modern racism.

What advice can an African American historian of religion offer white Christians and Jews about converting themselves from a compensatory liberalism that actually supports racial division? First, I would propose that white Christians disavow Professor Banfield's "Unheavenly City" and seek a truer vision of God's holy land. The vision must be de-multiculturalized by both Christians and Jews, because multiculturalism in America has been an oxymoron as far as African Americans are concerned—a historic contradiction. This contradiction exists because the churches that have recently been promoting the idea that God wants this country to be a multilayered, multicultural society have not yet paid their dues to the black people. They have, at the same time that they have been championing multiculturalism, given theological approbation to the domination of whites over blacks.

Until white religionists openly confess the sins of the distant past and take the lead in dealing with the blatant ideological and material injustices against the African American minority, I would propose that they take the Reverend Mather's quote and turn it on its head, so that it reads as follows:

> Come hither and I will show you, an Un-admirable Spectacle! 'Tis an Unheavenly City. . . . A City inhabited by an Innumerable Company of race despisers, and by the spirits of racists and unjust men and women. . . .

Take Off These Ungodly and Inhumane Garments of Racism, O America,
For You Yet Remain an Unholy City of Ungodly Prejudice.

Questions for Thought and Discussion

1. Would you agree or disagree that in the late twentieth century there has been a resurgence of racial bigotry in this country?

2. Discuss whether the church has had a role in shaping and sustaining racism.

3. Discuss the statement "History books have seduced many into believing."

4. Discuss whether you observe positive changes in the racial attitudes of many white Christians toward ethnic persons.

5. Discuss "multiculturalism" and whether it brings a glimpse of hope for the future.

7 | Why Apartheid Was Evil and Unbiblical

Desmond M. Tutu

I MUST HAVE met Gayraud Wilmore for the first time in 1972 on my first visit to the United States. I had just been appointed to the staff of the Theological Education Fund of the World Council of Churches (WCC). I was attending a consultation on Black Theology and African Theology at Union Theological Seminary in New York City, or it could very well have been at the Accra meeting of the WCC's Commission on Faith and Order of whose Standing Commission Professor Wilmore was a distinguished member. Whichever it might have been, I know that I was immediately struck by this quiet-spoken person who had an impressive incisive intellect and yet had an engaging manner. I fell under his spell from the first moment.

Gayraud Wilmore, perhaps unbeknownst to him, became my mentor in things theological as I learned how theology had to be an engaged theology dealing with the issues that were urgent for those of God's people who seemed to be His stepchildren. It could not be merely an academic enterprise, but would deal with burning questions about a proper theology for blacks suffering the anguish of blatant racism. Many at the time scoffed at the very notion of a Black Theology, and I and many others were greatly assisted in the existential task of making sense of our faith in a hostile environment by the outstanding contributions of Gayraud Wilmore, one of the founders of Black Theology in the United States. Thus, when asked to contribute to this volume, I happily complied with this chapter, which was originally presented in a slightly different form in a series of lectures I gave in Southeast Asia in 1995.

The Irony of the Early Mission Period

They tell the story of how, when Western missionaries came to Africa, we had the land and they the Bible. Then they said, "Let us pray," and dutifully we shut our eyes, and when the prayer was finished and we opened our eyes—why, they had the land and we had the Bible! Now that would have seemed to be a very bad bargain, that we were saddled with the thin edge of the stick. And yet, did it turn out to be such a bad bargain after all?

No, and several times no, because we discovered that we had been given a priceless treasure, the Word of God, by people whom we should honor warmly.

Many of them left comfortable homes to venture across the oceans to go to exotic, unknown lands braving a daunting danger and challenge.

It was through the Western missionaries' selfless devotion and commitment and zeal to preach the good news and to make disciples of all people that many of us are alive today through the outstanding medical missions they established, which provided a caring and healing ministry among the disadvantaged majority of the land when these people were being neglected by their government. The reason many of us are educated at all is because of the magnificent schools and colleges the missionaries set up. There would have been no education to speak of among black people in my country had it not been for the remarkable work of these men and women from overseas. Almost all the leaders of the liberation and decolonization movements have been educated in church-related institutions, and we must express profound gratitude and appreciation for this. Perhaps one of the reasons why black South Africans have been so ready to forgive and seek reconciliation with their former oppressors is because of the influence of the Christian church on them. At least, that is what one of them told a gathering of our bishops not long ago.

And what value can we attach to receiving the glorious and saving good news of the love of God which the missionaries came to preach and for our having become members of the body of Jesus Christ and temples of the Holy Spirit? This is something of inestimable worth, and we must give thanks to God for their consuming zeal to proclaim that good news.

And equally wonderfully they brought us the Bible, which turned out to be the most subversive, the most revolutionary thing you could ever have placed in the hands of those who were victims of racist injustice, oppression, and exploitation. The South African government was wont, in the bad old days of apartheid's vicious repression, to ban this or that piece of literature because in their view it was likely to sow bad thoughts of insurrection and revolution in the otherwise docile minds of their quiescent and kowtowing Natives (as we were then called, among other things). We were often able to say to that government and its minions that they were too late. The book that they should have banned long ago was the Bible. No political manifesto, not even the Marxist manifesto, turned out to be as revolutionary as the Bible in situations of injustice and oppression. Thus we were able to do theology authentically, relevantly, and contextually.

The Theological Struggle Against Apartheid's Racism

For a very long time there had been those in South Africa who thought they could provide a theological and biblical support for the ridiculous policy of apartheid. They would often use the story of the Tower of Babel in Genesis 11 as a proof text that God intended to have the various races of the earth separated.

We pointed out that this was perverse exegesis in the extreme. They were interpreting a biblical text completely out of its context.

The protohistory that these stories of the beginning time in fact indicated was that God's pristine intention had been for all His creation to live in harmony. That, surely, was one of the points of the story of the Garden of Eden, where there was no bloodshed, not even for the purposes of sacrifice, that human beings and animals lived, or had been intended to live, in peace and friendship, and that this idyllic state had been shattered by the intrusion of sin. Sin was described as fundamentally divisive and alienating. Adam and Eve quarreled; they hid from God and were separated from their Maker when previously God visited them frequently to walk with them in their garden in the cool of the day. There was enmity between Adam and the animal world because henceforth he would want to crush the serpent's head and it would seek to bruise his heel. Things were now out of joint, the earth now brought forth weeds instead of only plants. And Adam and Eve, as a result of the sin of their disobedience, were expelled from paradise.

It would be a very strange exegesis that then declared that this expulsion and their sojourn outside of paradise in a state of alienation and brokenness was in fact God's intention for them. It was equally perverse to say that the confusion of tongues and the scattering of the peoples who could no longer understand one another and thus could not create community, that this sad state of affairs that was God's punishment for the sin of human pride in trying to scale heaven itself, was God's intention for humankind. It was to ignore the entire thrust of the divine activity depicted in the Bible, the ingathering of all the peoples and the healing of the breach between God and his creation—the quest for the primal harmony that had been God's dream from the beginning. Herman Gunkel described it all in the phrase *Endzeit ist Urzeit* (the end time is as the beginning time). It is to ignore what St. Luke thought had happened in the first Christian Pentecost (Acts 2), where he depicts those momentous events, in part quite deliberately, as a reversal of what had taken place at the Tower of Babel. There the nations had sought to attack heaven. In Acts, they were gathered in Jerusalem on earth in obedience to God's decree about the Feast of Ingathering. Luke gives a list of nations who spoke different languages and then were able to hear and understand the good news preached. There they had dispersed out of confusion; here they were assembled, gathered together. There they had been unable to understand one another. Here the stress is on the fact that they did, for they heard the one proclamation in their different languages. There they were scattered as enemies. Here they came together to form a new community, the Christian community.

In addition, we were able to point out to the proponents of apartheid that the Bible and Christianity contradicted their racism at other critical points.

Human Worth Is Intrinsic

Apartheid, like racism everywhere, isolated an arbitrary biological attribute and asserted that this was what invested people with worth. Since from the nature of the case not everyone could possess this particular quality, it means that an elite was immediately created in which the group would be able to enjoy rights and privileges for which its members had not striven, and for which they were not necessarily qualified on other grounds except through the accident of birth. Anyone outside this privileged group could not hope to be admitted into its hallowed circle, no matter how hard he or she tried or how much he or she achieved. Exclusion and admission had nothing to do with merit or ability. They had everything to do with the accident of birth about which they really could do nothing. People were, as it were, praised or blamed for something they could do nothing about.

Apartheid said that what gave people worth was their ethnicity—their skin color. Since not everybody could be or was white, this worth would therefore not be a universal phenomenon. Even someone as clever as Aristotle had made a fundamental error in that he had declared that human personality was not a universal phenomenon, since slaves were not persons. It might not have mattered too much if many white people thought as the proponents of apartheid believed. You could dismiss it as you dismiss the ludicrous views of those who maintain in the face of all the evidence that the earth is not round but flat. Unfortunately, racist views have not been as innocuous in their consequences for the victims. As we are all aware, it was racism that gave the world the awful system of slavery. It was racism that caused the viciousness of the Holocaust. It was racism that was responsible for the lynchings and bombings in the Southern states of the United States. And, of course, apartheid was racism, and we know what suffering it inflicted on God's children totally unnecessarily. Racism cannot be just another political option available to be chosen by decent people. It is something we should all want to oppose with every fiber of our being.

It was wonderful, therefore, to say to the people who were being told that they did not count, who had their dignity callously trampled on underfoot daily, who were nonentities in the land of their birth, that they did count, that they were of infinite worth. The Bible and Christianity contradicted the assertions of apartheid and racism. They taught that what invested each and every human being with worth, with infinite value, was not this or that extrinsic attribute, particularly not a biological irrelevance. No, it was the fact that we were created in the image of God. This had nothing to do with birth, status, achievement, or whatever. It belonged to all human beings without exception. It was truly universal. It was a staggering claim to make about puny, fragile, vulnerable human beings. In olden days, the monarch could not be in every part of his domain simultaneously and so statues in the king's image were erected in all parts of the kingdom. His subjects were expected to give the same obeisance and reverence to the statue as to the monarch himself. Thus, to be designated as created in the image of God was to claim that we each were God's viceroys, stand-ins, representatives. Could anything be calculated to be more subversive, more likely to overthrow an unjust and repressive system than this knowledge—that we were created for something better, something more noble than to be the victims of injustice and oppression?

Contradicting Apartheid's Propaganda

I used to say to members of my Soweto congregation, most of whom were not very important people in the eyes of the world, I used to say to the women-folk, most of whom were probably domestic workers in white households, "When they ask, 'Who are you?' say, 'I'm God's viceroy, I'm God's representative, God's stand-in.'" This was preaching the gospel relevant to the life situation of our people, and it invariably became political because that is the nature of our incarnational faith.

We were able to say to our people that they were tabernacles of the Holy Spirit. They were God's carriers. And therefore to treat one such person, the image of God, a child of God, as if he or she were less than this was not only evil, not only painful, but positively blasphemous, since it was like spitting in the face of God. We would describe apartheid as evil without remainder, as immoral, unbiblical, and un-Christian. As believers in the God of the Bible we had no option. Not to oppose racism, injustice, and oppression was to disobey God. It was not just a political matter. It was also a deeply religious one. It was possible to use the Bible and Christian doctrine to demonstrate how immoral and evil apartheid was when it taught that we were fundamentally irreconcilable, or that we human beings were made for separateness, alienation, and to be divided off into mutually hostile groupings, or that human beings were means and not ends, to be manipulated and used for some purpose however beneficial.

We were able to draw strength and hope for our people in the dark days of apartheid's repression when it seemed as if evil was on an unstoppable road to ultimate victory. We were able to show that God, our God, was one who characteristically chose to be on the side of the weak, the oppressed, and the marginalized, as he had shown in the paradigmatic event of the Exodus when God chose to be on the side of a rabble of slaves who had done nothing to deserve the divine intervention on their behalf. This proved to be an unchanging and enduring attribute of our God because constantly and throughout the biblical record there was the exhortation that God's people, God's special representative, the king should show a similar bias on behalf of the widow, the orphan, and the alien—those who in most societies tended to be the least important, the most marginalized, and the most without clout or influence (Leviticus 19, Isaiah 1, Psalm 72). The worship of God's people was designed to make them more god-like and this was demonstrated by how sensitive they were toward the plight of those who seemed to be God's favorites (Isaiah 58, Isaiah 1, etc.).

God's Bias as Shown in Jesus

In the New Testament, God shows a similar concern and bias because God's Son was born not in the splendor and glory of a royal palace, but in the poverty and squalor of a stable. His parents were not the high and mighty, but a village carpenter and a village lass who did not have enough influence even to be able to persuade an innkeeper to give them a decent room in which their first child could be born. It seemed as if God wanted to make a particular point, for the first to be told about this momentous event were not those whom the world regarded as important, but so-called ordinary shepherds. The important ones felt threatened by this birth, and when they heard about it, plotted to kill the babe.

No one is ordinary since everyone is God's viceroy. We used to say to our people, "You might not be V.I.P.s, but you are each a V.S.P.—*a Very Special Person.*"

This Jesus showed the same concern and bias. He upset the religious leaders of his day by the disreputable companions he chose as his company. He was accused of eating with publicans, sinners, and prostitutes. He declared that in the final judgment we will be asked not whether we prayed or went to church, but whether we fed the hungry, clothed the naked, gave water to the thirsty. This service to the least of Christ's sisters and brothers would be service to Christ himself.

God's bias on behalf of those who could not do things for themselves is shown wonderfully in his intervention on behalf of us sinners in our struggle against the Devil. This is what caused St. Paul to exult, "Whilst we were yet sinners Christ died for us!" This God, our God, was the same yesterday, today, and forever. Just as he had heard the cries of the Israelites in bondage, just as he had seen their plight and knew their suffering, so also he heard and saw and knew our suffering. Just as He had come down to deliver the Israelites out of bondage, so he would come down to deliver us. Often we said these words at desperate times in our history—after massacres, at mass funerals when our people were near despair—and the message of the Bible brought us comfort and hope.

People who were suffering were often able even to laugh at themselves at such moments. We told them that their God did not give good advice at a safe distance, but was the same God who, when Shadrach, Meshach, and Abednego were thrown into the fiery furnace, preserved them when a fourth figure joined them. Our God came down and joined us in our anguish and distress. We recounted the story of Elijah's contest with the prophets of Baal when he taunted them, saying they should shout more loudly because perhaps their god was deaf, or sleeping, or busy, or had gone to the toilet. We could say that our God was always available. Our God did not go on holiday or was ever too busy to attend to them.

We pointed out that the Bible was quite realistic. In the Revelation of St. John the Divine there is the vision of the souls under the altar who cry out, "How long, O Lord?" meaning how long would the unjust prevail. The answer expected would be *not too long*. In fact, the Bible shows its stark realism by pointing out that before the vindication of the just could happen many more of their sisters and brothers would be killed. We used this story to stop our people from entertaining unrealistic expectations. We said that before apartheid was destroyed many of them would be detained. But we were able to assure them that the outcome was not in doubt. Jesus Christ, by his death and resurrection, had overcome evil and had shown that light is stronger than darkness, that life is stronger than death, that love is stronger than hate, and if God be for us, who can be against us?

We have won a spectacular victory over evil, apartheid, injustice, and oppression. We thank God for this victory and all our friends who have prayed for us, who have supported us and cared for us. Our story gives hope to the world—that if the nightmare of South African apartheid could end, then all nightmares everywhere in the world will end. Nothing, no nothing, can separate us from the love of God in Jesus Christ.

Questions for Thought and Discussion

1. Discuss the role of Western missionaries in various parts of the world, and particularly Africa.

2. How has the Bible been used to provide theological and biblical support for ridiculous policies?

3. Describe a situation where different languages contributed to or hindered the hearing and understanding of the gospel message.

4. What do apartheid and racism have in common?

5. How have politics influenced the church's agenda?

8 | The Quest for Holiness

Catherine Gunsalus González

GAYRAUD S. WILMORE was the Presbyterian staff person for the Student Christian Movement in the Middle Atlantic Region when I was an undergraduate at a college near Philadelphia in the early 1950s. He brought to that role an uncommon ability to think theologically and to also help students do so. His central concern seemed to be who we Christians were as the church in the world and how we understood ourselves and our world from that perspective. He believed it was important to know our own tradition and to be able to present its strengths to the rest of the church family. Beyond that, an ecumenical perspective joined us all together in a common task. Gay Wilmore presumed that all of us were capable of theological thinking as the source of our actions—even a young woman majoring in home economics. For many of us, black and white, men and women, he gave us the model and the support to begin our self-understanding as Christians and together to know ourselves part of the one, holy catholic church. It is out of that background that this chapter is offered.

Renewal movements often manage to reduce their central affirmations to three virtues. Paul managed to do that with the gospel: faith, hope, and love. The monastic movement has been summarized by the ideals of poverty, chastity, and obedience. Even the French Revolution was epitomized by the virtues of liberty, fraternity, and equality. This chapter holds that the particular genius of the Benedictine movement in monasticism can also be described by a triple set of virtues: stability, holiness, and moderation. Moreover, these particular virtues may have much to say to church life as a whole today.

Different Settings But Some Commonalities

The United States at the close of the twentieth century is very different from Rome in the sixth century. Here, the nation in which the church finds itself dominates much of the economic, social, and political life of the globe. In that earlier time, the Western Roman Empire was in the process of being destroyed. Cities and towns had been conquered and sacked, and would be again and again in the years to come. Wars raged over the countryside, destroying food supplies. Famine and disease were frequent. In the midst of this situation a movement was born that would be a major factor in the creation of a new culture that we call European. It was a new culture, but it joined the strengths of the Romans that had gone before it with the cultures of the Germanic groups that dominated the area. The movement was Benedictine monasticism. Even in our radically different situation, it has much to teach us.

Our nation's power and wealth are neither permanent nor evenly distributed. In many areas of the United States, both urban and rural, chaos reigns. Old political and social institutions no longer work. Enormous economic changes are occurring that displace workers and lead millions to the brink of despair. This chapter seeks to show the relevance of the major features of the Benedictine movement to our contemporary church life.

The Major Figures

Saint Benedict obviously is the primary figure in the form of monasticism that bears his name. It is a truism that St. Benedict is the "father of Western monasticism." The mother, however, was the church as it found itself in the midst of a chaotic world. When Benedict wrote his directions for monastic life— *The Rule*—about the year 539, invasions by the Germanic tribes had ended the Roman Empire in the West, and its glory had disappeared. The city of Rome itself, at its height several centuries before, had supported a population of more than a million. By the sixth century, the time of Benedict, the city was rapidly approaching its low point of only thirty thousand persons. War, famine, disease—all had taken their toll.

Benedict was born around 480, the son of a well-to-do family. He received a good Roman education. He was a devout Christian, but unhappy with the lack of seriousness with which most other Christians lived their lives. He sought, therefore, to become a monk, living in a cave in the hills near Rome. Many were such monks in the region, but word soon spread that this one was special. Others came to him for advice and to seek to be his disciples in the monastic life. Out of such experiences he finally wrote his *Rule*, outlining the ideal of monastic life as he had come to understand it.

Benedict was joined in his labors by his sister, St. Scholastic, who became the head of a group of women who lived under Benedict's direction.

Earlier forms of monastic life had been brought into the West from the Eastern church, but none had developed dominant indigenous forms. Benedict adapted these earlier streams, but added to them his own genius, strongly reflecting the characteristic elements of Roman culture. He wrote *The Rule* as a guide for others, at their request. It was not his intention to create a formal order or organization. Yet what he put forth sheds light on what it means to be a Christian community, even a nonmonastic one. Because of his efforts, monasticism became a means to the renewal of the church, since in his *Rule* he developed basic understandings of the nature of the Christian life that could apply to the whole church.

Benedict clearly was responding to the disintegrating social setting. He gave up the idea of being an isolated monk in favor of the formation of communities of monks, largely self-sufficient, growing their own food. The monastery provided a haven, a place of refuge, hopefully, from the world outside that was increasingly chaotic. If that were the whole purpose and end of the model it might have indicated that withdrawal from society is an appropriate way for the church as a whole to live out its life. But that was not the Benedictine monastery's purpose or end. Even in his days as a hermit, Benedict preached to the surrounding population, many of whom were not Christians. The monastery itself was to be an hospitable place for visitors and guests. The poor also could obtain food from its kitchens.

The social engagement of Benedictine monasticism was dramatically enhanced by the first monk to become pope: Gregory the Great, Pope Gregory I. Gregory was a Roman, the son of a very wealthy noble Christian family. He was born about 540, around the time that Benedict wrote his *Rule*. He was educated to be a civil official and held high office when only a young man. The Benedictine ideal strongly captured Gregory's imagination, so he gave up his wealth to become a monk. In fact, he gave his inherited estates for the purpose of establishing monastic houses where monks were to live under the Benedictine *Rule*. He himself joined one of these monasteries, refusing to be its superior. However, his ability as a leader, a problem solver, and a diplomat could not be obscured, especially in a time when such talents and experience were sorely needed by the whole society. He was often called out of his monastic retreat to perform services for the papacy, especially leading a delegation to the imperial court in Constantinople where he asked for aid in the worsening political and military situation in Italy. By popular demand and force of circumstances, he became the next pope, against his own wishes. As a pontiff, he used Benedictine monasticism as an agency of mission, establishing monasteries in non-Christian areas— as models of Christian communities—with the permission of the leaders of the people. The monasteries rendered services to the communities, especially medical and educational services. Often they became the nucleus around which towns developed. Men and women from the area became converts and joined these monastic communities. Thus, Benedictine monasticism became a city set on a hill, a light to the Gentiles, the proclaimer of the gospel. Other forms of monasticism would probably not have been able to accomplish this particular mission. The Benedictine form could do so precisely because of its character, which engendered the dominant, underlying theological perspectives that were to become the great gift of Benedict to the church, the trilogy of stability, holiness, and moderation.

Stability

Benedict stated in the prologue to his *Rule* that his purpose was "to establish a school for the Lord's service" (Prol. 45).[1] It was clear to him that Christians needed training in order to become true disciples. In his day, as in ours, the church outside the monastery frequently overlooked this basic task. It seems indisputable today that if a local church assumes its members are already so developed in their discipleship that no further nurture is needed, then that congregation has failed at a major point. Other organizations can assume that joining and perhaps paying annual dues are sufficient, but that is not the case with the church. The church is a school for discipleship, and no one graduates from it in this life.

All the rest of Benedict's *Rule* is his process for increasing the discipleship of those who have joined the monastic order. He established the novitiate—the period of trial and preparation before the individual and the community decided that joining was appropriate. Monastic life before Benedict was somewhat fluid. A person could join a monastery, decide that the superior was unfair, leave and join another. Benedict brought in the concept of "stability of residence." This meant that once a person joined one house, after an appropriate trial period, he or she could leave that house only by leaving monastic life altogether. Such a person could not join a different house. There were regulations that permitted the original house to receive the person again, but the practice of wandering from one monastery to another was brought to an end.

In our own day, there are those who treat the local congregation much as wandering monks treated the monastery before Benedict. They complain about the congregation to which they belong, and seek another. Never content that any house lives up to their expectations and demands, or that too many expectations are placed on them, they are never fully committed to any community of faith.

Commitment takes time and energy. In commitment one gives up the luxury of being a judge and takes on the role of member and participant. Granted, in a mobile society such as ours, it is often necessary to move. Church membership, therefore, must also change as one moves from one locale to another. There are also serious occasions that provide good and sufficient reasons to change from one congregation to another in the local community, even from one denomination to another. But what Benedict meant by stability remains critically important. We have many judges in our congregations. What would happen if the congregations they try to move had Benedict's view of the need for commitment and permanence? That would imply that churches neither attempt to em-

---

1. All references are given in the standard divisions of Benedict's *Rule*. The edition I am using is *The Rule of St. Benedict*, edited by Timothy Fry, O.S.B. (Collegeville, MN: The Liturgical Press, 1981).

brace them nor become gleeful when members of other congregations seek to join them. Serious questions would be raised about why those seeking membership had the wish to change congregations. In Benedict's view, people who move from one religious community to another because of problems they encounter, often take the problems with them to the new situation. "Stability of residence" was a major innovation in monastic life. It would also be an innovation in church life today. Behind the concept of stability lay some profound theological assumptions that are the heart of Benedict's contribution.

Also, Benedict's view of the need for preparation and trial before actually joining a monastery has relevance for us today. In fact, a similar emphasis has begun to take hold in many churches. A decade ago, most congregations welcomed new members readily. If someone indicated that they wished to join the church, perhaps after years of being away from any church life or even having never been involved as an active congregant, many congregations would be prepared to baptize or receive such a person in a few days or weeks. It was generally assumed that everyone born and raised in this society knew what the church believed. If people were willing to state their acceptance of these beliefs, then there was no reason to probe further. Nor was there seen to be much difference between decent social behavior and what the church taught. There was no need to require careful consideration about adding this person to the congregation, nor was there a need for the person wanting to join to consider the ramifications of such a commitment. In the past several years this pattern has changed, both in the Roman Catholic Church and in many Protestant churches. There is a new awareness that Christian values are not the same as normal civil decency. Church leaders seem more aware of the need to understand what the church teaches and believes. All this militates against casual membership. Furthermore, many denominations and congregations have developed strong adult education resources, precisely because of the need felt for enhanced discipleship. The contemporary church has discovered that it lives in mission territory. Gregory the Great's use of Benedictine communities in his mission to the Germanic groups may well be a model for our church life today.

Holiness

What lies at the heart of Benedict's stress on stability is his understanding of holiness. Holiness cannot be totally individual because it has so much to do with personal relationships. Only those who live in community can really learn where they need to grow in love, patience, and in all the qualities 1 Corinthians 13 points to as the heart of the Christian's holy life. Loving the neighbor is far easier if we have no interaction with the neighbor. Stability of residence is tied to the understanding of what holiness is and how it is achieved.

For both the hermit of old and the radically individualistic Christian of the late twentieth century, holiness is thought of in personal terms. One can be holy privately. One can conduct one's life in a holy manner, even if there is little contact with other people. Benedict knew better. Holiness for him had to do with human relationships and, therefore, requires human community. Furthermore, we can assume we are loving and patient until we have frequent interaction with someone who tries our patience and is decidedly unlovable. Even then, we can believe that our response to that person is quite Christian until others in the community point out our shortcomings. These were the reasons why Benedict tied holiness to community and community to stability. Stability of residence made the individual live in the midst of a group of people who could not be avoided. Holiness was the Christian's learned behavior in such a closely knit community. Holiness included humility and love, without which there could be no Christian community. In fact, humility and love could only be learned in the midst of close association with other people. The search for individual holiness has a selfish ring to it. If the goal is the holiness of the community, then each person is part of the means to the greater holiness of every other member of the community. Moreover, the holiness of the community is for the sake of God's glory and mission, and not that of the community itself.

Our contemporary culture stresses the individual rather than the community; it discourages commitment and long-term relationships. The local congregation has suffered as much from this as has the institution of marriage. If neighboring congregations took the same disapproving view of easy moving from one church to another and stressed the purpose of commitment in the Christian life, real holiness would have a better chance of growing in all our churches.

Benedict assumed that the task of the monastery was to create a holy community, not merely holy individuals. It was for this reason that the monastic community could be a means of mission: a corporate witness to the true character of the Christian life. It could be a model and not only a verbal proclaimer. That, too, is a message to local congregations in our own time. Their witness cannot be only by word, or even by doing good in the wider society, as important as that is. What matters above all is how clearly the corporate life of the community of faith demonstrates the love and hope that it preaches. It is this above all that attracts the world. In fact, the best deeds in the wider society come from an overflowing of love that goes beyond the boundary of the congregation. Deeds done out of duty and those done out of love will not have the same effect. Within the Benedictine community, the holiness of life based on humility and love was learned both in actions toward the neighbor and toward God. Toward God, these twin virtues of humility and love led to worship and obedience to God's will. Toward the neighbor, it meant actions of love that served the neighbor without thought to either person's social status. No work was too menial; everyone took turns at various tasks for the good of the community. Prayer was not holier than serving the neighbor. Each had its necessary place in the quest for holiness. The Benedictine ideal was a life that included the work of praise to God in worship and the work of service to the community in providing whatever was necessary for the common life. Out of this common life, the community served the needs of others. No one in the community could be excused from either form of work, though the sick, the elderly, and the children were involved in accordance with their special limitations.

It must be remembered that Benedict's original form assumed that all members were laity. A monk might be ordained as a priest in order to function as such within the community, but the rules for such ordination, and the care that was taken to be sure the person continued as a member of the community with no added rank or privilege, were clearly spelled out (*The Rule*, 62:1–11; 60:1–9). This, too, can be instructive for our contemporary congregations. The relation between clergy and laity is a strategic point at which humility and love can be learned.

All Christians have the obligation and the privilege to worship God. The form of worship in a monastic community obviously can include much more frequent corporate gatherings than are possible for those who do not live in monasteries. But all Christians can learn from the general ideal of hallowing all time in the context of worship. The practice of daily morning and evening prayer in families, in workplaces, or even alone, but with the awareness of being part of a community of faith, creates such hallowing. What mattered to Benedict was that there should be no substitution of our work in worship for our service to the community, or the reverse. Neither form of work is innately holier than the other. No person can perform one and ignore the other.

Service to the community could take many forms. *The Rule* assumes a farming community with much work to do in order to provide the food needed for all. There was also the cooking and serving, the cleaning up, the taking care of the provisions, the keeping of the books, the caring for the sick, the teaching of the young, and the governing of the whole community. The abbot or abbess was elected, though it is not clear by whom within the community. Holiness of life and wisdom in dealing with others were the criteria, not age, rank, or anything else. If the purpose of the monastery was to help the whole community become holy, then the leadership had to be in the hands of those who had made progress in that direction and had the capacity to help others (*The Rule*, 64:1–2). Above all, the virtue of moderation was required "so that the strong have something to yearn for and the weak nothing to run from."

The same requirements would be useful in one of our congregations when electing church officers or calling a pastor. Benedict was right to stress the Christian community as the essential medium of Christian growth. He was also right in holding as equally important service to God and to each other, with an emphasis on the holiness of both kinds of service.

Moderation

For Benedict, moderation was a necessary counterpoint and adjunct to holiness, a reminder that becoming holy is a lifelong process. Moderation is patience in action, both with ourselves and with others. If the community is stable—that is, it maintains stability with constant interaction—then reproofs from others are expected. They are reminders that we have not yet attained perfection. For both those who give such reproofs and those who receive them, moderation is necessary. We are not to expect either of ourselves or of others that sinful ways of a lifetime can be overcome at once. Benedict believed that it is an act of proper humility to take into consideration our limitations and the limitations of others, particularly the elderly, the sick, and the children (*The Rule*, 37:1-3). He was aware that learning to live in community was hard to do, and some might have to be expelled. But even in those circumstances there was moderation, for such recalcitrant members could be allowed to return, even going through the process of disciplinary action more than once (28:1—29:3).

The Rule is filled with examples of moderation in regard to physical needs, whether it is the kind and amount of food (39:1-6), wine (40:1-6), work (48:1-25), clothing (55:1-15), or sleep (8:1-4). Such moderation is a reminder of our human condition, in contrast to some earlier forms of monastic life that took pride in extreme measures.

Without the context of the stable Christian community, however, moderation can readily become the enemy of holiness. Moderation can devolve into a rationale for remaining with the status quo, for putting up with injustice, for excusing the unholy actions of ourselves and others. "We are only human" is a cry of complacency, not of holiness. Moderation makes sense as a virtue only if we are headed toward the long-term goal of holiness, rather like the training of a long-distance runner. A community that sees itself as a school of holiness needs the benefit of moderation lest it become discouraged, or burn itself out in the short run. But without the stable community that is engaged in the long-term quest for holiness, moderation can readily become the servant of individualism, not being involved, not calling others to account, ignoring or brushing off the reproofs of others toward us.

What makes the difference in the quality or character of moderation is the presence or absence of a community of faith to which all are accountable. Yet this quality is missing in much of contemporary church life.

There is no way that a congregation gathering once a week for an hour can be a stable community in Benedict's sense. This is especially true if the congregation is drawn from a wide geographic area and members have little or no contact with each other in their daily lives. There is no accountability in such an arrangement. Small-town church life did create some stability, if church members lived their lives in constant association with one another in the community outside of the church. But modern urban society militates against stability in Benedict's sense. It is also important to consider that the perspectives by which others view our attitudes and behavior are quite limited, given the narrow spectrum of class and race from which many congregations draw their membership.

What can be done to create a modicum of stability in this setting? Covenant groups, small prayer groups, neighborhood gatherings of church members during the week—all seek to address this issue. A stable Christian community requires a significant and consistent time commitment. The Benedictine monastic community guaranteed this, but it is not entirely unattainable today. One can imagine neighboring congregations across ethnic, economic, and denominational lines, seeking ways of being in communion with each other. Covenant or neighborhood groups could draw members from more than one congregation. Even more helpful, two congregations might covenant together to have members of their decision-making bodies attend each other's meetings to reflect on how one church's concerns look to fellow Christians with different perspectives. This is one way of calling each other to accountability over an extended period of time. It would only be useful, however, if the congregations agreed that neither was yet completely holy and that holiness was the goal toward which they both strove as individual entities. In such a context, both would have to practice humility, both would need to learn to love, and moderation in Benedict's terms would be exceptionally helpful.

Stability, holiness, moderation: These are the particular characteristics of Benedict's vision of the Christian community. It is clear that each of the three characteristics constantly points to the other two. The church of our own day is not a monastery, nor should it become one. But Benedict's insights are instructive nonetheless. If he is right about the nature of the Christian life, his trilogy will aid us in diagnosing some of the problems in our contemporary church life. As we have seen, we are often deficient in sustaining stable communities, and we lack, therefore, the kind of accountability we need. Growth in holiness is not always the stated goal of congregational life. Moderation we often excel in; but when moderation is not in the service of holiness, it can become demonic. The quest for holiness in the midst of a stable community can also become demonic without moderation.

Having a perceptive diagnosis for our ills as contemporary congregations is the starting point for renewal. In addition, Gregory the Great's contribution should not be left aside. A Christian community that is truly functioning as Benedict intended—not yet completely holy but where people are diligently working on it together—is the greatest missionary witness the church can have. It worked in the midst of the chaos that accompanied the fall of the Roman Empire. It might very well work in the chaos of our own neighborhoods today.

Questions for Thought and Discussion

1. Describe a "disintegrating social setting."
2. Do you agree or disagree that Christians need training in order to become true disciples? Why or why not?
3. Discuss the phrase "Commitment takes time and energy."
4. Why do people move from one religious community to another?
5. What adult-education resources does your congregation offer?
6. Describe someone who "tries our patience and is decidedly unlovable."

9 | Realism and Hope in American Religion and Race Relations

Gayraud S. Wilmore

I WANT FIRST to express my appreciation to the contributors to this volume. Over the years one receives many emoluments of one kind or another, some deserved and others gratuitous, for services rendered to the church and the academy. By the grace of God I have had my share from both institutions, and I am grateful for them all. None, however, gives more pleasure to me and the Wilmore family than this book, which—in the hope that long after our name has faded from memory—may still be collecting dust on a shelf of some sequestered library, waiting to be peered into by inquisitive researchers curious about all the fuss we made.

To comment on the interesting and provocative insights contained in these pages would be a challenging and even presumptuous enterprise for someone who has broader skills and considerably more energy than I. Some of what these good brothers and sisters have said about me here are patent exaggerations, but were, I'm sure, written out of a good faith and generous spirit. I accept them with humble gratitude. Other expressions and opinions in the foregoing pages have to do with areas of knowledge and praxis with which I have been absorbed most of my life, and represent the spheres of the ministry that Lee Wilmore and I have pursued in the Presbyterian Church, the ecumenical movement in the United States and abroad, and in my own writing and teaching hither and yon. About those statements of these friends and former students, I have both "Amens" to say and some arguments, but the arguments—academic and meager at best—must remain unstated in this final chapter, which is supposed to bring the book to an end. If I am forgiven for not commenting on the chapters individually, I want to say something different here, something that will, perhaps, sum up all the rejoinders I might have made to these distinguished contributors; some concerns that I have tried to express in recent years; and some ideas that may suggest where my mind is now, in retirement from more than fifty rich and busy years since I started out to become a minister of the gospel.

Before I present the essence of a lecture I gave at Lincoln University in 1995 as my humble contribution to this book, I want to express my thanks to the Rev. Dr. Eugene G. Turner, who is the editor of this book. Although it was another friend, J. Oscar McCloud, whose initiative at the 1994 annual meeting of the National Black Presbyterian Caucus gave wings to the idea of honoring me in this way, it was Gene Turner who finally took up the cudgels, worked on the final edition of the papers, queried the publishers, and saw this effort through to its conclusion. Gene, who was my student and avid supporter in the sometimes hostile classrooms at Pittsburgh Seminary where I began my teaching career, welcomed my advice (as a grumpy old editor who always had difficulty keeping his blue pencil off of other peoples manuscripts but usually missed errors in his own!) and did all the hard work that makes a book possible. Thanks once again, Gene! I hope your readers will judge the effort kindly and one that they deem worthy of the time and effort you expended at a critical time of transition in your own career.

* * * *

During the school year 1995–1996 I accepted an invitation from Dr. Niara Sudarkasa, the president of Lincoln University in Pennsylvania, my alma mater, to be the Thomas H. and James R. Amos Scholar, in honor of the first two graduates of Ashmun Institute (which later was renamed Lincoln University). These first two graduates went to Liberia together in 1859 as the first black Presbyterian missionaries from the United States. On the occasion of the public lecture that was held in the Mary Dod Brown Memorial Chapel on November 15, 1995, I presented a paper that Lincoln has granted permission for me to revise and offer as my contribution to this book. Of all the articles and addresses I have written in the past year or two, this, I think, best represents my continuing and still maturing belief that by means of unblinking realism, activist scholarship, and open and honest debate in the public square, we can move with integrity and assurance toward the liberation and reconciliation the world so desperately needs, and without which the Church of Christ could not subsist.

I

For a twenty-four hour period in August 1995 an unusual gathering was called together at the Interdenominational Theological Center in Atlanta. Twenty-five veterans of the Civil Rights movement—now gray-haired men and women, black and white, and, at this particular meeting, all Presbyterians—met to reminisce about what we did and failed to do in the revolution of the 1960s. It is fair to say that we senior citizens represented the most militant leadership of one predominantly white, middle-class church—the Presbyterian Church (U.S.A.)—during that period. A church that, taking many social scientists by surprise, had actually spent millions of dollars helping to fund the Civil Rights movement between 1963 and 1973—paying the salaries of such leaders as Hosea Williams on Dr. King's staff; getting people to demonstrations like the March on Washington in 1963; running freedom schools and voter-registration projects in Hattiesburg, Mississippi; bailing black and white protesters out of Southern jails; dispatching urban specialists into riot-torn cities like Newark and Watts to help people who had been made hungry and homeless by the burning; and providing funds for the legal defense of such political prisoners as Angela Davis and Cesar Chavez. By now it can be well documented that the Presbyterian Church disturbed the peace of both Negroes and whites who were at ease in Zion while millions who happened to be black, or red, or Hispanic, suffocated under a blanket of legalized racial, ethnic, and class—not to mention gender (which we were least aware of during the time)—discrimination.

Twenty-five of us came together in Atlanta, not so much to slap each other on the back and revel in the memories of marching with Dr. King or getting arrested for picketing county courthouses in Mississippi, but to sit around a large table and try to reconstruct the history of our movement. A history that, because most secular historians tend to ignore the role of the churches, will be lost forever if some of us who worked for religious organizations during those days do not take pains to record what happened from our point of view.

I was asked to transcribe the audiotapes of that meeting and to produce a book that, when it is published, will describe the contributions that black and white Presbyterians made to the gains that some younger people of both races are enjoying today, or will enjoy when they graduate from colleges and graduate schools and get into the world where our battles were fought.

What I wanted to do in the third annual Amos Lecture was not turn a spotlight on the specific actions we were involved in, although that would have made an interesting discussion, but rather to reflect on the role of religion and religious people in the quest for racial justice in the United States. Many would agree that the complicity of Western Christianity in perpetuating racism, since the beginning of the Atlantic slave trade, has been so disgraceful and so distressing that if anyone can attribute something positive to religion, the academic community needs to know about it. Well, that was my purpose in the original lecture and in this chapter. Too few educated people know that in the second half of this century, some men and women of the church played an unprecedented part in the struggle for freedom. I want to peruse that role, not to justify it, or use it to compensate for the racism that, sad to say, still abounds in most white churches, but to ask this question: What was the significance of religion in the effort for racial equality during the past fifty or more years? Moreover, what can we learn about the relationship between religion and race during the 1960s and 1970s that may help us turn back the current right-wing assault on whatever progress we may have made?

II

Let me start with this thesis statement: What we call Christian race relations began during the 1940s with three assumptions on the part of the mainline white denominations: (1) that by designating a Race Relations Sunday every February and getting out some literature on the desirability of interracial contact between congregations, we could expect to create a nonsegregated church before the year 2000; (2) that church-sponsored social action for nondiscriminatory policies in housing, employment, education, and places of public accommodation would put such a dent in racism that, in addition to a nonsegregated church, we would also create a nonsegregated society; and (3) that both of these much heralded prophecies could come to pass without radically disturbing the basic status quo, that is, the normal flow of traditional political, economic, and cultural transactions on which this nation rests. That is to say, we Christians might rock the boat, but we wouldn't have to turn it over, to capsize it in the process.

When, in the middle of the 1960s, this wishful thinking proved to be a sad miscalculation, a wave of cynicism, disillusionment, and programmatic retrenchment broke out across the normally placid surface of the denominational bureaucracies. Those of us who worked in the churches experienced an angry white backlash against any fundamental change in the nation's or the church's posture. In response to this backlash, the African American churches suddenly reverted to a new hardness on their part, an unsentimental realism that produced a new radicalism, a black theological revolution in both the academy and the church that has not yet played itself out.

Today the once well-heeled church "religion and race" establishments have been reduced to only a shadow of their former splendor, and even in the black churches one scarcely finds any interest in efforts for racial harmony and reconciliation—although that situation is slowly changing.[1] However, most churches, both white and black, still sit gloomily on the sidelines of the secular world, watching in dismay while the structures of interracial cooperation crumble all around us. Today relations between white and black believers in this country—and here I include Christians, Muslims, and Jews—have sunk to the lowest ebb since the turn of the century.

As far as American Protestantism is concerned, the first stage of religion and race began during my boyhood, and Lincoln University, at that time a Presbyterian institution, played an interesting part in it. When I was still a student at Central High School in Philadelphia, I attended one of the famous Lincoln University summer conferences sponsored by the Institute for Racial and Cultural Relations of the Presbyterian Church. This unit of our church had responsibility for race relations. Its annual summer conferences gave white and black church people an opportunity to meet, sleep, talk, and eat together on the lovely tree-shaded campus of Lincoln University, where we could sit on the grass in

---

1. I recently co-chaired a workshop on racism that brought out more than a hundred Atlanta Presbyterians on a cold, rainy November night. The majority were African Americans, eager to discuss racism against the background of the O. J. Simpson verdict and the Million Man March. Five years ago there may have been ten or twelve people in all, and mostly white. This new interest is rising, I'm told, all over the country today.

circles and entertain each other with stories about how we first became aware
of our racial phobias and prejudices. I have fond memories of the "Lincoln Summer Conferences" as an opportunity to get to know white Christians in a way
that had not been possible in North Philadelphia, where we had to fight Irish
Catholic boys almost every day in order to get access to the playgrounds and
ball fields of Fairmount Park.

When we met with whites on Lincoln's campus during the 1930s, race relations meant playing footsy across the color line, experiencing the warm fuzzi-
ness of interracial fellowship. But that was as far as it went. In his book *Church
People in the Struggle: The National Council of Churches and the Black Freedom Movement, 1950–1970*, James F. Findlay, Jr., writes the following:

> That approach left the decisions about the pace of change in the hands of
> whites, which usually meant little or no change. It was also a point of view
> fully in tune with the public temper of the early fifties. Education and face-to-
> face discussion could be useful first steps toward change, but in themselves
> offered no long-term solutions to such deeply entrenched structural prob-
> lems in the society as poverty or segregated housing and public schooling, all
> of which inevitably accompanied discrimination and enabled the latter to re-
> main deeply rooted in our national life.[2]

In 1946 the Federal Council of Churches called for a "nonsegregated church
and nonsegregated society," a mandate that sought to integrate local congregations as the first step toward breaking down the granite wall of racial separation, but it turned out to be primarily an attitudinal change strategy. It didn't
take us long to realize that integration would require considerably more than
new attitudes cautiously evoked at church camps and summer conferences. Experiencing a season of genial fellowship at Lincoln, Fisk, and other black colleges during the summer months, or even some token integration in a few
congregations like Howard Thurman's Church of All Nations in San Francisco,
might have made a few of us feel better, but it had little or no effect on the in-
tricate problem of racism in America.

By the time the 1950s rolled around, the churches realized they had to be
more realistic about race relations if their good intentions were to produce anything worthwhile. Presbyterians were the first to introduce a more hardheaded
approach. Between 1956 and 1960, I was a member of the staff of the Department
of Social Education and Action of the Presbyterian Church in Philadelphia, and
participated enthusiastically in the change of emphasis from the attitudinal
change conferences of the 1930s and 1940s to strategies specifically designed
to influence social, economic, and political policies and practices. Public statements on the ethics of desegregation, writing letters to elected officials, lobbying
in state capitols and in Washington, D.C., suddenly took the place of sitting on

2. James F. Findlay, Jr., *Church People in the Struggle: The National Council of Churches and
the Black Freedom Movement, 1950–1970* (New York: Oxford University Press, 1993), p. 19.

the grass at summer conferences and exchanging guilt feelings about our prejudices. By the later 1950s we were beginning to use the material resources of
the church to combat "institutional racism" rather than only personal prejudices. Timidly at first but later more boldly, we brought ecclesiastical pressure
to bear against legal barriers to integration, to work for equal job opportunities,
open housing, and voting rights. Congregations and regional judicatories set up
social-action committees that were supposed to ensure that employers, realtors,
and other gatekeepers of the society made racial justice a normal part of doing
business. Religion, we thought, was finally getting with it—finally cutting some
ice with the movers and shakers of the society. But that came mainly after
Montgomery, after 1955.

Unfortunately, our earlier efforts were too little and too late. When the Supreme Court handed down the Brown vs. Board of Education decision on
May 17, 1954, it was obvious that instead of leading the civil order in abolishing
racism, the religious community had only been following—and mostly at a distance. The next year a young Baptist minister in Montgomery, Alabama, named
Martin Luther King Jr. saved the churches from further embarrassment by leading fifty thousand citizens, organized by black ministers, in a nonviolent bus
boycott that launched the most significant mass movement in the history of the
nation.

In the summer of 1963, my church called me from a teaching post in social
ethics in Pittsburgh Theological Seminary to become the first executive director
of its new Commission on Religion and Race, with offices on the eighth floor of
the bustling Interchurch Center in New York City. Black Presbyterians, some of
the most prominent of whom were Lincoln men—for example, Frank T. Wilson,
Jesse Barber, Milton Galamison, Leroy Patrick, Frank Gordon, Robert T.
Newbold, Robert Shirley, and Maurice Moyer—applied the pressures that led
to the creation of the Commission on Religion and Race.[3] This unit had the
strongest mandate of any church race-relations agency in the nation, an annual
budget of a half million dollars, and a national and regional interracial professional staff. Among all denominations, black or white, none made a greater effort after 1963 to catch up with and support Dr. King than did the Presbyterian
Church.

At a recent celebration of the twenty-fifth anniversary of one of the Presbyterian mission programs, a former Student Nonviolent Coordinating Committee
(SNCC) leader and the author of the Black Manifesto, James Forman, said that

---

3. The pressure came from a caucus of black Presbyterians at the Des Moines General
Assembly where Dr. King had been invited to speak. When he was unable to come, Dr.
Edler G. Hawkins, pastor of St. Augustine Presbyterian Church in the Bronx, took his
place, and a movement was launched to bring the church into the center of the struggle
by creating the Commission on Religion and Race.

"of all the churches, the Presbyterians were the only ones who gave a damn."[4] That may be a slight exaggeration, but the Presbyterians led white Protestantism generally into a new stage of religion and race relations in which the vocabulary shifted from "combating racial bigotry" and "promoting attitudinal change" to "working for racial justice" and "reforming the social, economic, and political structures of American society."

Beginning with the historic Chicago Interfaith Conference on Religion and Race in January 1963, the churches—Protestant, Roman Catholic, and Jewish— changed their target from prejudice in churches and synagogues to institutional racism in the society at large. Some influential church leaders like Martin Luther King Jr., and Eugene Carson Blake[5] were saying, "Later for personal attitudes and integrated congregations—the first order of business now is direct action against unjust laws."

But it's important to note that this shift of focus landed the churches in a completely different arena, one where they would have to accept bedfellows they had not slept with since the Prohibition Era, when zealous evangelicals, working across denominational lines, succeeded in getting the nation to accept the 18th Amendment to the U.S. Constitution in 1920. Not only was something missing in the 1960s, in terms of a personal and spiritual dimension for the struggle, but once again the churches were engrossed in a complex web of politics, and if you know anything at all about politics you'll understand what that meant. Politicians, for the most part, act on the basis of compromise and expediency rather than moral absolutes. When religious institutions descend to that level of politics, as they must if they are serious about operating in the real world, they have to pay a price that is usually more than they bargained for.

III

After religious institutions, following Dr. King, adopted the new strategy of direct action and began to manipulate the dangerous levers of power, they had to accept the possibility of being blown away. Actually the black churches had long understood the volatility of politics and religion and, as Benjamin Quarles pointed out, had never been squeamish about mixing the two since before the Civil War.[6] Although our black denominations did not mount the kind of centralized and coordinated racial justice strategies in the 1960s that the

---

4. Forman's Black Manifesto was issued by the Black Economic Development Corporation in April 1969 and demanded five hundred million dollars in reparations from American churches and synagogues for two hundred years of black slavery.

5. Blake was the Stated Clerk of the United Presbyterian General Assembly, the highest administrative office in the denomination, and also president of the National Council of Churches, without a doubt, the most prestigious Protestant churchman in the nation.

6. Benjamin Quarles, *Black Abolitionists* (New York: Oxford University Press, 1969), p. 81.

white denominations sponsored, they had long before grown accustomed to political action. In fact, our churches had been aggressive about black survival and liberation since the period immediately following the American Revolution. For black Methodists and Baptists, political action was inseparable from being a church. What C. Eric Lincoln wrote in the Foreword of the first edition of my *Black Religion and Black Radicalism: An Interpretation of the Religious History of Afro-American People* has been true for 95 percent of African Americans who call themselves Christians:

> Their church was their school, their forum, their political arena, their social club, their art gallery, their conservatory of music. It was lyceum and gymnasium as well as *sanctum sanctorum*. Their religion was the peculiar sustaining force that gave them the strength to endure when endurance gave no promise, and the courage to be creative in the face of their own dehumanization.[7]

Most blacks, those within the white churches as well as those in the historic black churches, were not surprised, therefore, at the punishing backlash that came from white Christians when the basic pattern of religious social concern shifted from attitudes to direct action, from the use of moral suasion to the use of political and economic sanctions, or to put it more baldly—when the paradigm shifted from white power to black power. We had all been there before.

It is one of the ironies of American church history that at the very time when the seams of highly educated, sophisticated, and affluent white churches were unraveling over direct action and they were in such theological disarray as to be unable to keep their laity engaged in hard political struggle, the poorly educated, unsophisticated black churches were awakening to a new black theology that advocated political action for the liberation of the oppressed. And moreover, they recognized such action as the very heart and soul of the gospel.[8]

This transition of American theological leadership from white to black actually began with the ministries of two black religious leaders—Martin Luther King Jr. and El Hajj Malik El-Shabazz, the name Malcolm X adopted for himself after deciding that the Civil Rights movement had significance for Islam after all. Malcolm said to James Booker of the *New York Amsterdam News* following his expulsion from the Black Muslim movement: "I'm throwing myself into the heart of the civil rights struggle and will be in it from now on."[9]

Thus, without consciously collaborating, black Christianity and black Is-

---

7. Gayraud S. Wilmore, *Black Religion and Black Radicalism: An Interpretation of the Religious History of Afro-American People* (Maryknoll, NY: Orbis Books, 1995), p. vii.
8. See James H. Cone and Gayraud S. Wilmore, *Black Theology: A Documentary History, 1966–1992*, 2nd ed. (Maryknoll, NY: Orbis Books, 1993).
9. Cited in James H. Cone, *Martin & Malcolm & America: A Dream or a Nightmare* (Maryknoll, NY: Orbis Books, 1991), p. 2.

lam together helped to radicalize the movement for racial justice by evolving a loosely organized religious wing of the Black Power movement. In this way, by 1967, they had supplanted and marginalized the coalition of liberal white denominations that sponsored the Commission on Religion and Race of the National Council of Churches and supported Dr. King. Those white denominations, including my own, were paralyzed by the backlash of their laity against James Forman's Black Manifesto and its raucous call for reparations.

Both King and Malcolm accepted political and economic power as a realistic and legitimate means for changing America. By 1969, with both leaders dead, the Black Power movement gave birth to a new theology developed initially by two African American academics who mirrored both the polarities and the symbiosis between King and Malcolm—James H. Cone of Union Seminary in New York City and J. DeOtis Roberts, at that time a professor of theology at the Divinity School of Howard University in Washington, D.C. Instead of the Southern Christian Leadership Conference (SCLC), which showed little interest in following up on the more radical side of King's intellectual legacy, the new theology found a vehicle in the National Committee of Black Churchmen (NCBC), and later in the Black Theology Project of Theology in the Americas, and the Society for the Study of Black Religion.[10]

IV

Looking back from the lowlands of 1995, I think it's fair to say that the impotence of the white liberal churches after 1968, hobbled by the growing conservatism of their laity and unable to appreciate the significance of the black Christian dissent and empowerment as a theological datum, forced Black Theology into existence. While the white churches were able to tolerate King as long as he avoided openly supporting the Communist party or criticizing the war in Vietnam, they were not able to accept the implications of the new theology, which not only made political action the cornerstone of its Christian realism, but attempted to transvaluate the whole corpus of Christian doctrine in order to make it more relevant to the masses of black people.

Black theology was more appreciated by European than by American theologians. The German theologian Helmut Gollwitzer made the case that black theology, by emphasizing suffering and struggle for liberation of the oppressed, was the only theology of this century qualified to speak to the masses. For

---

10. The National Committee of Black Churchmen was a northern-based clergy organization, founded in 1967. The salary of its executive director was paid by the Commission on Religion and Race of the Presbyterian Church. For a fuller identification of these groups, see "General Introduction," in *Black Theology: A Documentary History, 1966–1979*, edited by Gayraud S. Wilmore and James H. Cone, 1st ed. (Maryknoll, NY: Orbis Books, 1979), pp. 1–12.

Gollwitzer, the new theology that evolved from the writings of Cone, Roberts, and a remarkable array of young African American theologians and church leaders, was the only authentic Christian theology to address the political and cultural implications of sin and salvation in the American context.

Gollwitzer criticized what he called the apathetic and unproductive activism of mainline white Christianity and accused it of failing to draw from the biblical roots that were being tapped by bombed-out and burned-out black churches.

> The pain-shy white activism is not replaced by a corresponding black activism. The profound black experience of the not only dehumanizing, but also humanizing power of suffering, is drawn into that time when all sufferings and humiliation will have been terminated. This cannot be preached to suffering and battling colored humanity from the outside, from the side of whites; they can only be suspected of ideology. But the black Christians who are battling along with colored humanity, equipped with the message of Jesus' cross and resurrection, are sent to the brothers and sisters to help them stay clear of the repetition of white sins. . . . If our motive in the political liberation battle is the obedience to the Gospel of God's liberation struggle on the political level, and if we ask God for his blessing, that is, that he identify himself with our struggle and through it pursue his work, it still makes for a difference if God identifies himself with us or we identify with him.[11]

Gollwitzer was saying that because of their realism, their acceptance of nitty-gritty political struggle, the African American churches, for the most part, had remained true to the gospel by grounding activism in a transcendent hope mediated by the life, death, and resurrection of Jesus, rather than by any assumption of racial self-righteousness. It would not have been possible to say the same thing of the white churches of America at that point in time.

A Japanese-American woman, explaining why her people celebrated the Fourth of July while being held in internment camps during the Second World War, said that they never lost faith. Under persecution, she said they learned something crucial about themselves. "We need," she wrote, "to leave our legacy to our children. And also our legacy to America, from our tears, what we learned."[12]

What a beautiful way to put it—"*our legacy . . . from our tears, what we learned.*" That is the profound vocation of the black church and black theology: to pass on to successive generations, "*from our tears*" in the midnight hour, from our suffering and struggle in slave baracoons and urban ghettos, "*what we learned.*"

And what did we learn? Mainly, we learned what it means to be human;

---

11. Helmut Gollwitzer, "Why Black Theology?" in Wilmore and Cone, *Black Theology,* pp. 168–169.

12. Cited by Linda R. Monk, in the *Atlanta Journal and Constitution,* July 2, 1995.

to affirm ourselves as children of God against every power that would rob us of that identity; we learned what it means to fight for the liberation of human beings from bondage to every form of repression and degradation; we learned how to combine Christian love with secular justice and secular realism with Christian hope.

These are lessons of history and the Bible that some white Christians remembered in the radical 1860s, but that many were too timid or too lacking in faith to put into practice in the 1960s. Nor have they shown much sign of recovering those lessons in the 1990s. Perhaps it is now the peculiar responsibility of the black church and the black academy to preserve that understanding of religion and to continue applying it to the relationship between races, classes, and genders. But we cannot and ought not try to do it on our own. Others must take a share of this ministry. The African American churches and academic institutions have their own sins and need to be reminded to repent of them even as they call for repentance from friends and allies.

V

It is not possible to delve into all the complexities of the religious efforts for racial justice between 1963 and the death of King in 1968. The main point I want to make is that during my lifetime, racial-justice programming in the churches went through a sea-change that can be largely attributed to a combination of realism and hope, dissent and empowerment in a black movement that occurred, of all places, within the predominantly white Presbyterian Church! We have not fully exploited the positive accomplishments of Christian race relations in several denominations during that period, nor shall we do so until we retrace the road over which we have all come these past fifty years. The white denominations entered the 1940s with an attitudinal change theory that was transmuted into a structural change praxis that was effective in helping to get the Civil Rights Act of 1964 and the Voting Rights Act of 1965 enacted into law, but they did not seem to realize that true progress in race relations could never be sustained without radical changes in the economic and political systems of this country, and without a voluntary, or if necessary, an *involuntary* transfer of some of the wealth and power of those on the top to those on the bottom.[13] This they were not prepared to do. The greatest disappointment of white Christians was that black brothers and sisters with whom they reclined on the grass and traded folksy stories at the Lincoln summer conferences came to believe that

---

13. This was the message of Forman's Black Manifesto which was initially presented for endorsement to a conference at Wayne State University called by the Interreligious Foundation for Community Organization. Black Presbyterians played a major role in that conference and its sensational aftermath.

it was necessary to give poor people the means of power, to demand extreme remedies, to march in the streets, and to refuse unqualified loyalty to the values of a crassly capitalistic economy.

Today—with a resurgence of racism occasioned by the Simpson verdict and the Million Man March—it is necessary for those who believe in the truth and power of religion to try to mend the connective tissues between blacks and whites, tissues that were torn by the assassinations of Malcolm and Martin on the brink of their ideological convergence, and then broken decisively by the misunderstood and inadequately implemented Black Power movement. The mistakes of the past, on all sides, need to be acknowledged and corrected before a wave of racial and religious hatred breaks out in the nation that will make the eruptions of the Civil Rights period look like a playground scuffle.

We did not meet long enough in Atlanta that summer for all our hindsight to surface, but I sensed that many of the Civil Rights veterans who sat around that table in the Costen Center were prepared to accept more blame for the white backlash than we were disposed to accept thirty years ago. When you don't have the reins firmly in hand, it is better not to push your horse too hard or too fast if you want to stay in the saddle. Most of us were, after all, terribly young, but we were also biblical Christians. Perhaps we should not have been so enchanted by the secular forces with which we were allied that we forgot the Word of the Lord to Zerubbabel: "Not by might, nor by power, but by my spirit, say the LORD of hosts" (Zech. 4:6).

On the other hand, those black churches that stood on the sidelines when they should have been in the center of the struggle, and those white churches that melted before the torrid wave of reaction in the pews and pulled back from affirmative action against racism, also must shoulder some of the blame for the retrenchment that we are experiencing today.

Can the religious community find its way back to the interracial cooperation, to the political realism and Christian hope that characterized it during the four or five years before Dr. King's assassination? I don't know, but it is clear to me that the forces that have captured American religion today—and here I speak particularly of the mainstream black and white churches—want to ignore the pluralistic, multiethnic character of the society and force the whole nation into the mold of the Christian Right—the religious wing of the Republican party that intends to subordinate the justice goals of prophetic religion to a privatized religiosity that blames the victims.

When we look at the aggressiveness with which the Christian Coalition of Ralph Reed and Pat Robertson is attacking the gains of the Civil Rights movement, we know that even if some of us find it too difficult and distracting to worship together on Sunday, we who profess the faith of the Bible must come together during the rest of the week and resist this mean-spirited, misguided attempt to turn the hands of the clock backward in the name of the Lord.

Yet this fight must not expunge from our hearts the vision of multicultural churches, synagogues, and mosques that can lead us to an interreligious and interracial unity that takes the place of competition and divisiveness without watering down our individual differences. Realism and hope can help us, whether we are Christians, Jews, or Muslims, black or white, male, female, or something in between, to prioritize our energies for universal justice and peace under the specific conditions of where we live, work, and worship the one God who is the Creator and Lord of all.

At the risk of sounding like Bill Clinton in that famous speech he gave at the University of Texas in October 1995, I conclude with the observation that most of the hopelessness we feel is not because of the loss of that exalted vision of one global community of brothers and sisters, but to the loss of communication between us. We exist today in a dangerous state of noncommunication. To be more specific, we are not sharing our separate perceptions of what it means to be black and white, Christian and Muslim, at the end of the twentieth century.

We need a new, realistic, and theologically enlightened dialogue that honestly faces who we are, what we stand for, the reasons for our failures in the past, and a determination to mend fences and return to the struggle together. Neither an integrated church or mosque, nor a concerted attack on racism can occur if black and white believers are not talking to each other. But white Christians have to make the first move. The weight of error and wrong is on their side.[14] The future will depend not only on communication between us, but on white believers opening themselves to the contributions of a neglected and falsified history, culture, and religion that blacks want to bring to the table. At the same time, the future will depend also on blacks being open to the ongoing march of history—to the limits of a parochial and inflexible Afrocentrism in a world that has become much too small and too multicultural to be saved by any one race, ideology, or religion.

Here, I think, is where the religious heritage of Lincoln University comes in. The "God of Ethiopia," to use Cortlandt Van Rensselaer's, one of its earlier benefactors, famous phrase,[15]

> summoned Lincoln's first graduates, Thomas H. Amos and his brother James, to our ancestral land in 1859. Today, we can draw religious insight and inspiration from that early commitment of Lincoln to Africa and the African diaspora. It remains, however, for the faculty and students of every African American college, university, and theological seminary today to recover the broadest and deepest meaning of that religious inheritance, sadly atrophied

---

14. See one of the strongest recent confirmations of this view, in Nibs Stroupe and Inez Fleming, *While We Run This Race: Confronting the Power of Racism in a Southern Church* (Maryknoll, NY: Orbis Books, 1995).

15. Horace Mann Bond, *Education for Freedom: A History of Lincoln University, Pennsylvania* (Princeton, NJ: Princeton University Press, 1976), p. 214.

by years of neglect, and use to it to help all of us overcome the continuing estrangement between races, classes, and genders, developed and developing nations, and between the church, the mosque, and the academic community.

Questions for Thought and Discussion

1. Discuss this statement "The mistakes of the past, on all sides, need to be acknowledged and corrected before a wave of racial and religious hatred breaks out in the nation that will make the eruptions of the Civil Rights period look like a playground scuffle."

2. How is your church attempting to recover the broadest and deepest meaning of Africa and the African diaspora to the religious experience for African Americans?

Biographical Sketch of
Gayraud S. Wilmore

Gayraud S. Wilmore was born in Philadelphia, Pennsylvania, on December 20, 1921, the first offspring of Gayraud S. Wilmore, Sr., of Philadelphia and Patricia Gardner Wilmore of Gloucester County, Virginia. He attended Central and Ben Franklin High Schools and matriculated at Lincoln University, Pennsylvania, in January 1940, but was drafted into the U.S. Army in his sophomore year. While in the service, in 1944, he married the former Lee Wilson of Atlanta and Philadelphia. He saw action on the Italian front as a radio operator with the 92nd Infantry Division during the Second World War. When the war in Europe ended, he briefly attended the University of Florence in Italy and later completed his undergraduate studies at Lincoln, graduating with highest honors with a B.A. in 1947. In 1950, he was first in the graduating class of the Lincoln University Theological Seminary (B.D.) and while serving as pastor of the Second Presbyterian Church of West Chester, Pennsylvania, earned the Master of Sacred Theology from Temple University's School of Religion in Philadelphia.

After being called from the pastorate in 1953 to become Regional Secretary of Student Christian Movement in the Middle Atlantic Region, he later joined the staff of the Presbyterian Board of Christian Education in Philadelphia and began doctoral studies in social ethics at Drew Theological Seminary. He was able to transfer his studies to Temple after being appointed an assistant professor in social ethics at Pittsburgh Theological Seminary (1959–1963), but his doctoral studies and seminary teaching career were interrupted in the crisis-ridden summer of 1963 when the United Presbyterian Church called him to become the first executive director of the newly created national Commission on Religion and Race.

The Commission was the first denominational racial-justice program established to cooperate with Dr. King after the historic interfaith Conference on Religion and Race which met in Chicago in January 1963. From 1963 to 1972 he led this national program of the Presbyterian Church, headquartered in New York City and serving in Hattiesburg, Mississippi, and in major cities across the nation during the northern city rebellions. In 1972 he left the church's racial-justice bureaucracy to become Martin Luther King Jr. Professor of Social Ethics at Boston University School of Theology, but the Civil Rights movement had whetted his interest in African American religious history, and when he left in

1974 to join the faculty of the Colgate Rochester Divinity School in Rochester, New York, he began to teach church history. Until retirement in 1990, he was Professor of Church History at the Interdenominational Theological Center (ITC) in Atlanta, Georgia. In addition to social ethics and American church history, he has taught African American religious history, black theology, and the history of African Americans in the Presbyterian Church. Prior to coming to the ITC in 1988, he was Academic Dean and Professor of African American Religious Studies at New York Theological Seminary (1983–1988), and before that, Martin Luther King Jr. Professor of Black Church Studies at Colgate Rochester Divinity School (1974–1983). He holds honorary doctorates from Lincoln College, Illinois; Tusculum College in Greenville, Tennessee; Lincoln University, Pennsylvania; Payne Theological Seminary at Wilberforce, Ohio; General Theological Seminary in New York City; and Trinity Lutheran Theological Seminary in Columbus, Ohio. He was the first recipient of the Sower Award of the New York Theological Seminary in 1988, and in 1995 received the Edler G. Hawkins Award of the National Black Presbyterian Caucus for meritorious service to the church. He was selected Distinguished United Negro College Fund Professor for 1986 and has been a visiting professor at the ITC, Princeton Theological Seminary, Payne Theological Seminary, the Pacific Lutheran Theological Seminary, Southern Baptist Theological Seminary, and Lutheran Theological Seminary in Philadelphia. For several years after retirement he was an adjunct professor in the Doctor of Ministry Program of United Theological Seminary in Dayton, Ohio.

Dr. Wilmore was one of the founders of the National Committee of Black Churchmen (NCBC), the Pan African Skills Project, and the Black Theology Project of "Theology in the Americas."

While in Boston he was editor of *The Black Church*. He has been a contributing editor of *The Christian Century* and the former *Christianity and Crisis*. Until 1994, he was editor of the *Journal of the Interdenominational Theological Center* and the ITC Press. He was a member of the original editorial board of the Lenten Booklet *Liberation and Unity*, now published by the Consultation on Church Union.

Gayraud S. Wilmore has lectured in the United States, Europe, Africa, Asia, and the Caribbean. His writings have appeared in numerous books, encyclopedias, and scholarly journals within and outside the United States. His best-known work, *Black Religion and Black Radicalism: An Interpretation of the Religious History of Afro-American People* (Maryknoll, NY: Orbis Books, 1983), is in its tenth printing and was slated for a third revision by Orbis Books in 1997. Among nineteen other books, authored or edited, are *Black and Presbyterian: The Heritage and the Hope.* Revised and Enlarged Edition (Louisville: Witherspoon Press, 1997); *Last Things First* (Philadelphia: Westminster Press, 1982); *The Secular Relevance of the Church* (Philadelphia: Westminster Press, 1962); *Black Witness to the Apostolic*

Faith, with David T. Shannon (Grand Rapids: Wm. B. Eerdmans Publishing Co., 1988); and *African American Religious Studies: An Interdisciplinary Anthology* (Durham: Duke University Press, 1989). He edited three ITC Press books, *Black Men in Prison: The Response of the African American Church* (1990); *Reclamation of Black Prisoners: A Challenge to the African American Church* (1992); and *From Prison Cell to Church Pew: Strategy of the African American Church* (1993), the last two with Gloria Askew. He co-edited with James H. Cone the two-volume *Black Theology: A Documentary History*, published by Orbis Books in 1993 and widely used as a seminary textbook.

He was a founder and past president of the Society for the Study of Black Religion (SSBR); a board member of the Black Religious Studies Network (BRSNET), a computer network linking scholars and pastors involved in African American Religious Studies; a member of the Society of Christian Ethics, the American Academy of Religion; and a consultant to the Kelly Miller Smith Institute, a black religious research center at Vanderbilt University.

He is a life member of the NAACP, and for many years was the representative of the Presbyterian Church (U.S.A.) on the Standing Commission of the World Council of Churches' Commission on Faith and Order. In that capacity he chaired the 1983 international consultation in Geneva which produced the WCC study "Racism in Theology and Theology Against Racism." He is also a founding member of the Ecumenical Association of Third World Theologians (EATWOT).

Notwithstanding long and faithful service to the African American church and community, as a minister of a predominantly white denomination, Gayraud S. Wilmore's life's work has consistently emphasized peacemaking, justice, and reconciliation between racial and ethnic groups in the United States and abroad.

The Wilmores have had four children, three boys and a girl. The youngest, David Luther, is deceased. Three adult children now live in Massachusetts and Virginia and have given their parents four grandchildren. After retirement from the ITC, Gay and Lee continue to make their home in Atlanta, Georgia.

About the Contributors

James H. Cone is the Charles A. Briggs Professor of Systematic Theology at Union Theological Seminary in New York City. His first book, *Black Theology and Black Power* (Seabury, 1969), is considered the seminal work in African American theology and religious scholarship in the United States. Among his several books is the widely used, two-volume anthology he co-edited with Gayraud S. Wilmore, titled *Black Theology: A Documentary History, 1966–1992* (Orbis, 1993). Professor Cone is a founding member of the Society for the Study of Black Religion (SSBR) and the Ecumenical Association of Third World Theologians (EATWOT).

Bryant George was associate executive secretary of the Board of National Missions of the United Presbyterian Church and worked for the Ford Foundation during the Civil Rights period. Today he serves as a consultant for Counterpoint Foundation in Washington, D.C. Upon retirement from government service he received the Philippines Presidential Medal of Merit and AID's Distinguished Service Award. He presently serves on the staff of the New York Avenue Presbyterian Church in Washington and continues to travel widely for the U.S. State Department.

Catherine Gunsalus González is a professor of church history at Columbia Theological Seminary in Decatur, Georgia. She is an ordained minister of the Presbyterian Church (U.S.A.) and serves on many national boards and commissions of her denomination and of the National Council of Churches. She is the author of *Lea and Gregory: Shapes of the Church* (Graded Press, 1988) and *A Faith More Precious Than Gold: A Study of 1 Peter* (Horizons, 1989) with her husband, Justo L. González.

Paul R. Griffin is a professor and head of the Department of Religion at Wright State University in Dayton, Ohio. An ordained minister of the African Methodist Episcopal Church, he taught church history at the Payne Theological Seminary, the A.M.E. seminary in Wilberforce, Ohio, before going to Wright State as Assistant Professor of the History of Religion. He is the author of *Black Theology as the Foundation of Three Methodist Colleges: The Educational Views and Labors of Daniel Payne, Joseph Price, and Isaac Lane* (University Press, 1984) and *The Struggles for a Black Theology of Education: The Pioneering Efforts of Post Civil War Clergy* (ITC Press, 1993).

Thomas L. Hoyt, Jr. was elected the 48th bishop of the Christian Methodist Episcopal Church in 1995 after a distinguished career as a professor of New Testament at the Interdenominational Theological Center (ITC) in Atlanta, Howard University School of Religion in Washington, D.C., and Hartford Theological Seminary in Hartford, Connecticut. He is a highly regarded ecumenist at national and world levels and one of the primary architects of the group of black biblical scholars whose annual meetings at Collegeville, Minnesota, produced the pathfinding *Stony the Road We Trod: An African American Biblical Interpretation* (Augsburg Fortress, 1991), edited by Cain Hope Felder.

T. Richard Snyder is academic dean and professor of theology and ethics at the New York Theological Seminary in New York City. He is an ordained minister of the Presbyterian Church (U.S.A.) and has served churches in Brazil, Philadelphia, and New York. He is well known as a social action, urban church, and racial-justice advocate in Presbyterian and ecumenical circles. He has been closely related as an instructor and administrator for the unique NYTS Master of Religious Studies degree program for inmates at Sing Sing, the New York State correctional facility. He is the author of *Once You Were No People: The Church and The Transformation of Society* (Meyerstone, 1988) and *Divided We Fall: Moving from Suspicion to Solidarity* (Westminster/John Knox Press, 1992), with a foreword by Gayraud S. Wilmore.

Desmond Mpilo Tutu is known worldwide for his efforts against apartheid in South Africa where, until his retirement, he served as the Anglican Archbishop of Cape Town. He has taught theology at the University of Botswana, Lesotho, and Swaziland, and was director of the Theological Education Fund of the World Council of Churches, based in Kent, England. He received the Nobel Peace Prize in 1984 and continues to work for peace and justice in the new Republic of South Africa that he helped to bring into existence. He has written *Crying in the Wilderness: The Struggle for Justice in South Africa* (Books on Demand, 1982), *Hope and Suffering* (Eerdmans, 1984), and is one of the founding members of the Ecumenical Association of Third World Theologians.

Delores S. Williams is the Paul Tillich Professor of Theology and Culture at Union Theological Seminary in New York City. Prior to coming to Union she taught theology at Drew University in Madison, New Jersey; Fisk University in Nashville, Tennessee; Harvard Divinity School, Cambridge, Massachusetts; and Boston University School of Theology. She is a leading proponent of Womanist theology in the United States and the author of one of the major works in the field, *Sisters in the Wilderness: The Challenge of Womanist God-Talk* (Orbis, 1995). With Katie Cannon, Beverly Harrison, Ada-Maria Azzes-Diaz, and Mary Pellaw, Delores S. Williams wrote *God's Fierce Whimsy: Christian Feminism and Theological Education* (Pilgrim Press, 1985). Professor Williams is a member of the Presbyterian Church (U.S.A.) and a widowed mother of four children.

About the Editor

Eugene G. Turner is the Associate Stated Clerk for Ecumenical Relations of the General Assembly of the Presbyterian Church (U.S.A.). He pastored in Pittsburgh, Pennsylvania; Paterson, New Jersey; and Philadelphia, and was a church executive in the Bay Area of California during the latter years of the Civil Rights movement. He was an adjunct professor in the Doctor of Ministry Program at San Francisco Theological Seminary from 1972–1973. He was the first synod executive of the Synod of the Northeast of the Presbyterian Church from 1975 to 1993 and is the author of *The Making of the Impossible Synod* (Synod of the Northeast Press, 1991). He is a frequent writer for the church press.

Selected Bibliography of Works by Gayraud S. Wilmore*

Wilmore, Gayraud S., editor. *African American Religious Studies: An Interdisciplinary Anthology*. Durham: Duke University Press, 1989.

———. "African and Black Theology—Ghana Consultation: A Summary Report," in *Journal of Religious Thought* 32 (Fall—Winter 1975): 104–109.

———. "Afro-American Religious Studies and Theological Education." *Journal of Theology* 43 (1989): 61–69.

———. "Awakened by Easter," in *Christianity and Crisis* 49 (March 20, 1989): 75–76.

———. Review of *Black American Politics: From the Washington Marches to Jesse Jackson* by Manning Marable, in *Christianity and Crisis* 45 (January 13, 1986): 548–549.

———. Review of *Black Americans and the Evangelization of Africa, 1877–1900* by Walter L. Williams, in *International Bulletin of Missionary Research* 9 (July 1985): 138–139.

———. "Black Americans in Mission: Setting the Record Straight," in *International Bulletin of Missionary Research* 10 (July 1986): 98–102.

———. *Black and Presbyterian: The Heritage and the Hope*. Revised and enlarged edition. Louisville: Witherspoon Press, 1997.

———. Review of *Black and African Theologies: Siblings or Distant Cousins?* by Josiah U. Young, in *International Bulletin of Missionary Research* 12 (April 1988): 77.

———. *Black and Presbyterian: The Heritage and the Hope*. Philadelphia: Geneva Press, 1983.

———. "Black Christians, Church Unity, and One Common Expression of Apostolic Faith," in *Black Witness to the Apostolic Faith*, edited by Gayraud S. Wilmore and David T. Shannon, 357–365. Grand Rapids: Wm. B. Eerdmans Publishing Co., 1985.

———, general editor. *Black Church Scholars Series*. 7 vols. Atlanta: ITC Press, 1990–1994.

———. Review of *Religious Leaders: Conflict in Unity* by Peter J. Paris, in *Christian Century* 95 (October 11, 1978): 963.

———. *Black Men in Prison: The Response of the African American Church*. Vol. 2. *Black Church Scholars Series*. Atlanta: ITC Press, 1990.

———. "The Black Messiah: Revising the Color Symbolism of Western Christology," in *Journal of the Interdenominational Theological Center* 2 (Fall 1974): 8–18.

———. Review of *Black Odyssey* by Nathan I. Huggins, in *New Review of Books and Religion* 2 (February 1978): 6ff.

———. "Black Pastors/White Professors: An Experiment in Dialogic Education." Special Issue 1. *Theological Education* 16 (Winter 1980): 83–169.

———

*Compiled by Dr. Joseph E. Troutman, Theological Librarian, Interdenominational Theological Center, Atlanta, Georgia, March 1994. Courtesy of the Woodruff Library, Atlanta University Center.

——. *Black Religion and Black Radicalism.* Garden City, NY: Doubleday, 1972.

——. *Black Religion and Black Radicalism: An Interpretation of the Religious History of Afro-American People.* 2nd ed. Maryknoll, NY: Orbis Books, 1983.

——. "Black Religion and Black Radicalism," in *Monthly Review: An Independent Socialist Magazine* 36 (July–August 1984): 121–126.

——. "Black Religion: Basic Themes and Orientations," in *The Sons of Sheba's Race: African Americans and the Italo-Ethiopian War,* edited by William R. Scott and William G. Shade.

——. "Black Religion: Strategies of Survival, Elevation, and Liberation" in *Journal of the Interdenominational Theological Center* 21 (Fall 1993/Spring 1994).

——. "Black Theology and Pastoral Ministry: A Challenge to Ecumenical Renewal and Solidarity," in *The Pastor as Theologian,* edited by Earl E. Shelp and Ronald H. Sunderland, pp. 30–67. New York: Pilgrim Press, 1988.

——. "Black Theology: Its Significance for Christian Mission Today," in *International Review of Mission* 63 (April 1974): 211–231.

——. "Black Theology of Liberation," in *Ministry Among Black Americans,* St. Meinrad, IN: St. Meinrad School of Theology, 1980.

——. "Black Theology: Raising the Questions," in *Christian Century* 94 (July 20, 1977): 645–646.

——. "Blackness as Sign and Assignment," in *Social Crisis Preaching,* edited by Kelly Miller Smith. Macon, GA: Mercer University Press, 1984.

——. "Brotherhood Month, 1963 [meditation]," in *Perspective* 4 (March 1963): 4–5.

——. "The Case for a New Black Church Style," in *The Black Church in America,* edited by Hart M. Nelsen, Raytha L. Yokley, and Anne K. Nelsen, pp. 324–334. New York: Basic Books, 1971.

——. "The Case for a New Black Church Style," in *The Black Experience in Religion,* edited by C. E. Lincoln, pp. 34–44. Garden City, NY: Doubleday Publishing Company, 1974.

——. "The Christian in Organization Politics" in *Social Progress* 50 (June 1960): 32–38.

——. "The Church and Theology in North America," in *Theology in the Americas: Detroit II Conference Papers,* edited by Cornel West, Caridad Guidote, and Margaret Coakley, pp. 90–96. Maryknoll, NY: Orbis Books, 1982.

——. *The Church's Response to the Black Manifesto.* New York: United Presbyterian Church, U.S.A., 1969.

——. "Connecting Two Worlds: A Response to James Henry Harris," in *Christian Century* 107 (June 13, 1990): 602–604.

——. "CORAR: The First Five Years," in *Presbyterian Commission on Religion, Church and Society* 78 (November/December 1987): 60–67.

——. "The Disturbing Ecumenism of the Black Church in America," in *Ecumenical Trends* 14 (September 1985): 113–115.

——. "Doing the Truth: Some Criteria for Researching African American Religious History," in *African American Religion: Research Problems and Resources for the 1990s,* edited by Howard Dodson and Victor N. Smyth, pp. 133–137. New York: Schomburg Center for Research in Black Culture, 1992.

——. Three articles on Black Presbyterian history, in *Encyclopedia of African American Culture and History,* edited by Jack F. Salzman, David Lionel Smith, Cornel West (Macmillan Library Reference, U.S.A.), 1996.

——. Three articles on Black Presbyterian history, in *Encyclopedia of African-American Religions*, edited by Larry G. Murphy, J. Gordon Melton, and Gary L. Ward. Garland Publishing Co., 1993.

——. "Ethics in Black and Blight," in *Christian Century* 40 (September 12, 1973): 877–878.

——. Review of *The Ethics of Martin Luther King Jr.* by Ervin Smith, in *Theology Today* 40 (July 1983): 212–218.

——. Review of *Frontiers of the Theology in Latin America* by Gustavo Gutierrez et al. Edited by Rosino Gibellini, in *New Review of Books and Religion* 4 (November 1979): 14–15.

——. "Good Reading," in *Christianity and Crisis* 50 (October 22, 1990): 313–314.

——. "The Historical Mandate for African American Theological Education," in *AME Church Review* 105 (April–June 1990): 60–71.

——. "Identity and Integration: Black Presbyterians and Their Allies in the Twentieth Century," in *The Presbyterian Predicament: Six Perspectives*, edited by Milton J. Coalter, Jr., John M. Mulder, and Louis B. Weeks, pp. 109–133. Louisville: Westminster/John Knox Press, 1990.

——. Review of *The Identity Crisis in Black Theology* by Cecil W. Cone, in *Union Seminary Quarterly Review* 32 (Fall 1976): 54–56.

——. "Inner City Seminaries," in *Christianity and Crisis* 52 (April 13, 1992): 118–120.

——. *Last Things First.* Philadelphia: Westminster Press, 1982.

——. "Letters to a White Liberal," in *The Wild Goose: A Journal for Liberal Ministry* 1 (September 1989): 22–38.

——. "Los Angeles: Peace or Pacification" in *Christianity and Crisis* 52 (May 25, 1992): 163–164. Editorial. *Winner of the Associated Church Press Award for Best Editorial in 1992.*

——. "The Negro Revolt," in *Social Progress* 54 (December 1963): 7–11.

——. "The New Context of Black Theology in the United States," in *Mission Trends*, no. 4, *Liberation Theologies*, edited by G. H. Anderson and T. F. Stransky, pp. 113–122. New York: Paulist Press, 1979.

——. "The New Context of Black Theology in the United States," in *Occasional Bulletin of Missionary Research* 2 (October 1978): 140–142.

——. "The New Need for Intergroup Coalitions," in *Christian Century* 99 (February 17, 1982): 170–173.

——. "The New Negro and the Church," in *Christian Century* 80 (February 6, 1963): 168–171.

——. "Open Letter to Vincent Harding," in *Cross Currents* 37 (Winter 1988): 468–472.

——. "Pastoral Ministry in the Origin and Development of Black Theology," in *Journal of the Interdenominational Theological Center* 13 (Spring 1986): 213–224.

——. "The Path Toward Racial Justice," in *Journal of Presbyterian History* 61 (Spring 1983): 110–117.

——. "Reinterpretation in Black Church History," in *Chicago Theological Seminary Register* 73 (Winter 1983): 25–37.

——. "Religion and American Politics: Beyond the Veil," in *Christianity and Crisis* 45 (April 29, 1985): 155–157.

——. "Religion and Philosophy of Black America," in *World Encyclopedia of Black Peoples,* edited by Keith Irvine, pp. 290–305. St. Clair Shores, MI: Scholarly Press, 1975.

———. "Report of the Theological Commission Project of the National Committee of Negro Churchmen," in *Christian Faith in Black and White*, edited by Warner Traynham, pp. 83–95. Wakefield, MA: Parameter Press, 1973.

———. Review of *The Return* by Yaw M. Boateng, in *New Review of Books and Religion* 2 (February 1978): 6ff.

———. "A Revolution Unfulfilled, But Not Invalidated," in *A Black Theology of Liberation: Twentieth Anniversary with Critical Responses*, edited by James H. Cone, pp. 145–163. Maryknoll, NY: Orbis Books, 1990.

———. Review of *A Rock in a Weary Land: The AME Church During the Civil War and Reconstruction*, edited by Clarence E. Walker, in *Theology Today* 20 (July 1983): 212ff.

———. "The Role of Afro-America in the Rise of Third World Theology: A Historical Appraisal," in *African Theology en Route*, edited by K. Appiah-Kubi and S. Torres, pp. 196–208. Maryknoll, NY: Orbis Books, 1979.

———. *The Secular Relevance of the Church*. Christian Perspectives on Social Problems Series. Philadelphia: Westminster Press, 1962.

———. "Selma: Memories and an Exhortation," in *Christianity and Crisis* 50 (March 5, 1990): 51–52.

———. "The Situation of Christian Pan Africanism in the U.S. Today," in *Journal of the Interdenominational Theological Center* 16 (Fall 1988/Spring 1989): 273–278.

———. Review of *The Social Teaching of the Black Churches* by Peter J. Paris, in *Journal of the American Academy of Religion* 54 (Summer 1986): 384–385.

———. "Some Contributions to Planning the Future of Theological Education," in *Theological Education* 11 (Autumn 1974): 48–49.

———. "The Spirit of Black Presbyterianism, 1807–1861," in *Periscope I*, edited by Clarence L. Cave. New York: Office of Black Mission Development, United Presbyterian Church, U.S.A., 1982.

———. "Spirituality and Social Transformation as the Vocation of the Black Church," in *Churches in Struggle: Liberation Theologies and Social Change in North America*, edited by William K. Tabb, pp. 240–253. New York: Monthly Review Press, 1986.

———. "Stalking the Wild Black Theologues," in *Social Progress* 60 (October 1969): 3.

———. "Steve Biko, Martyr," in *Christianity and Crisis* 37 (October 17,1977): 239–240.

———. "Survival and Liberation in Black Faith," in *We Are One Voice*, edited by S. Maimela and D. Hopkins, pp. 1–33. Braamfontein [South Africa]: Skotaville Publishers, 1989.

———. "Tension Points in Black Church Studies," in *Christian Century* 96 (April 11, 1979): 411–413.

———. "The Theological Dimensions of Black Presbyterianism," in *Periscope III*, edited by Clarence L. Cave. Louisville: Racial Ethnic Ministry Unit, Presbyterian Church, U.S.A., 1992.

———. "Theological Education in a World of Religious and Other Diversities," in *Theological Education* 23 (Supplement 1987): 142–164.

———. "Theological Ferment in the Third World," in *Christian Century* 95 (February 15, 1978): 164–168.

———. "The Theology of the Black Church," in *The National Assembly of Black Churches*, edited by James E. Hurt. New Orleans: CNBC, 1984.

———. "To Speak with One Voice: The Ghana Consultation on African and Black Theology," in *Christian Century* 92 (February 19, 1975): 167–169.

———. "Toward a Common Expression of Faith: A Black North American Perspective," in *A.M.E. Zion Quarterly Review* 158 (July 1985): 37–44.

——. "War and Christian Conscience: How Shall Modern War Be Conducted," in *Perspective* 2 (September 1961): 21–24.

——. "What Seeds, What Flowers?" *Christianity and Crisis* 53 (April 12, 1993): 86–87.

Co-Edited Publications

Wilmore, Gayraud S., and Gloria Askew, editors. *Reclamation of Black Prisoners: A Challenge to the African American Church*, by James H. Costen et al. Vol. 3. Black Church Scholars Series. Atlanta: ITC Press, 1992.

——, editor. *From Prison Cell to Church Pew: The Strategy of the African American Church*. Vol. 5. Black Church Scholars Series. Atlanta: ITC Press, 1993.

—— and James H. Cone, editors. *Black Theology: A Documentary History, 1966–1979*. Vol. 1. Maryknoll, NY: Orbis Books, 1979.

—— and James H. Cone, editors. *Black Theology: A Documentary History, 1980–1992*. Vol. 2. Maryknoll, NY: Orbis Books, 1993.

—— and James H. Cone, editors. *Black Theology: A Documentary History, 1966–1992*. Revised two-volume edition. Maryknoll, NY: Orbis Books, 1993.

——. "Black Theology and African Theology," in *Black Faith and Black Solidarity*, edited by Priscilla Massie, pp. 104–126. New York: Friendship Press, 1973.

—— and Richard A. Gilbert. "Fascism with a Friendly Face," in *Christian Century* 98 (August 26/September 2, 1981): 836–837.

—— and Choan Seng-Song, editors. *Asians and Blacks*. Bangkok: East Asian Christian Conference, 1972.

—— and David T. Shannon, editors. *Black Witness to the Apostolic Faith*. Grand Rapids: Wm. B. Eerdmans Publishing Co., 1988.

——. "Toward a Common Expression of Faith: A Black North American Perspective," in *Journal of the Interdenominational Theological Center* XIII (Spring 1986): 333–340.

Series Editorships

Black Church Scholars Series

Askew, Gloria, and Gayraud S. Wilmore, editors. *Reclamation of Black Prisoners: A Challenge to the African American Church,* by James H. Costen et al. Vol. 3. Atlanta: ITC Press, 1992.

——. *From Prison Cell to Church Pew: The Strategy of the African American Church.* Vol. 5. Black Church Scholars Series. Atlanta: ITC Press, 1993.

Griffin, Paul R. *The Struggle for a Black Theology of Education: Pioneering Efforts of Post Civil War Clergy.* Vol. 6. Atlanta: ITC Press, 1993.

Wilmore, Gayraud S., editor. *Black Men in Prison: The Response of the African American Church.* Vol. 2. Atlanta: ITC Press, 1990.

Christian Perspectives on Social Problems Series

Campbell, Will D. *Race and the Renewal of the Church.* Philadelphia: Westminster Press, 1962.

Cone, Arnold B. *Drinking: A Christian Position.* Philadelphia: Westminster Press, 1964.

Rasmussen, Albert Terrill. *Christian Responsibility in Economic Life.* Philadelphia: Westminster Press, 1965.

Robinson, James Herman. *Africa at the Crossroads*. Philadelphia: Westminster Press, 1962.

Seifert, Harvey. *Ethical Resources for International Relations*. Philadelphia: Westminster Press, 1964.

Wilmore, Gayraud S. *The Secular Relevance of the Church*. Philadelphia: Westminster Press, 1962.

Younger, George D. *The Church and Urban Power Structure*. Philadelphia: Westminster Press, 1963.